Navigating the Spectrum

A Comprehensive Guide to Autism

Ethan D. Anderson

Xspurts.com

A New Zealand Designed Product

Other Versions Available

Why limit yourself to just one format?

This book is now available in physical, digital, and audiobook options.

Choose the way you love to read and dive into the story today. You won't regret it!

Digital ISBN: 9781776968978
Physical ISBN: 9781776968961
Audio ISBN:

To obtain a different format of this book at a discounted price, please get in touch with us at:

http://isbn.xspurts.com/

Contents

Have Questions / Comments?

This book was designed to cover as much information as possible, but I know I have probably missed something, or some new amazing discovery has just come out.

If you notice something missing or have a question that I failed to answer, please get in touch and let me know. If I can, I will email you an answer and also update the book so others can also benefit from it.

Thanks For Being Awesome :)

Submit Your Questions / Comments At:

https://questions.xspurts.com

Get Free Stuff

We love writing and have produced a huge number of books.

For being one of our amazing readers, we would love to offer you more books we have created, 100% free.

To claim this limited time special offer, simply go to the site below and enter your name and email address.

You will then receive loads (as we love our readers so much :) of our great books, content and audio direct to your email account, 100% free!

Get Loads of FREE Stuff at:

https://free.xspurts.com

Chapter One

Understanding Autism

Autism Spectrum Disorder (ASD) is a complex neurodevelopmental disorder that affects an individual's social interaction, communication, and behavior. It is a lifelong condition that typically becomes evident in early childhood, with symptoms often appearing before the age of three.

Autism is a spectrum disorder, which means that it affects individuals differently, and to varying degrees. Some people with autism may have difficulty communicating or may exhibit repetitive behaviors, while others may have difficulty with social interactions or sensory processing. The severity of symptoms can also vary widely, from mild to severe.

The causes of autism are not fully understood, but research suggests that genetic and environmental factors play a role. Some studies have suggested that the disorder may be linked to prenatal exposure to certain toxins or viruses, while others have found evidence of genetic mutations that may contribute to the disorder.

One of the most common symptoms of autism is difficulty with social interactions. This may include difficulty making eye contact, understanding social cues, and engaging in reciprocal conversation. Individuals with autism may also have difficulty with imaginative play and may prefer solitary activities.

Communication difficulties are also common in individuals with autism. Some individuals may have delayed language development or difficulty with language comprehension. Others may have difficulty with nonverbal communication, such as facial expressions and body language.

Repetitive behaviors and routines are another hallmark of autism. Some individuals may exhibit repetitive movements or vocalizations, such as hand flapping or echolalia. Others may become fixated on specific objects or routines and become upset if these are disrupted.

Sensory processing issues are also common in individuals with autism. Some may be hypersensitive to certain stimuli, such as bright lights or loud noises, while others may seek out certain sensory experiences, such as spinning or rocking.

There is no cure for autism, but early intervention and therapy can help to improve outcomes for individuals with the disorder. Treatment options may include behavioral therapy, speech therapy, and occupational therapy, as well as medication to manage symptoms such as anxiety and depression.

Autism Spectrum Disorder: An Overview

Autism Spectrum Disorder (ASD) is a complex developmental disorder that affects social interaction, communication, and behavior. It is a neurological condition that typically appears in early childhood and affects people throughout their lives. The term "spectrum" in Autism Spectrum Disorder refers to the wide range of symptoms, abilities, and levels of impairment that people with ASD can experience.

The American Psychiatric Association's Diagnostic and Statistical Manual of Mental Disorders, Fifth Edition (DSM-5), provides the criteria for diagnosing ASD. These criteria include impairments in social communication and social interaction, restricted and repetitive behaviors, and interests or activities. The severity of these symptoms can vary widely, from mild to severe.

One of the key features of Autism Spectrum Disorder is difficulty with social communication and interaction. People with ASD may have difficulty making eye contact, understanding nonverbal cues, and developing relationships with others. They may also have difficulty understanding social norms and rules, which can lead to social isolation and difficulty in school and work settings.

Another feature of ASD is restricted and repetitive behaviors, interests, or activities. This can include repetitive movements or vocalizations, rigid routines or rituals, intense interests in specific topics or objects, and sensory sensitivities.

ASD is a complex disorder, and the exact cause is not yet fully understood. However, research suggests that both genetic and environmental factors may contribute to the development of ASD. Some studies have found that certain genetic mutations or changes in brain development may increase the risk of developing ASD. Other studies suggest that environmental factors, such as exposure to certain chemicals or viruses during pregnancy, may also play a role.

There is currently no cure for Autism Spectrum Disorder, but there are a variety of treatments and therapies available that can help people with ASD to manage their symptoms and improve their quality of life. These may include behavioral interventions, speech therapy, occupational therapy, and medication.

Early intervention is key in the treatment of Autism Spectrum Disorder. Many children with ASD benefit from intensive early intervention services that focus on building social, communication, and behavioral skills. Parents and caregivers can also play an important role in supporting their children with ASD by learning about the disorder, advocating for their children's needs, and seeking out appropriate services and supports.

As awareness of Autism Spectrum Disorder has grown in recent years, there has been a greater emphasis on inclusion and acceptance of people with ASD in all areas of society. This includes in education, employment, and community activities. People with ASD have a lot to offer and can make significant contributions to society when given the appropriate supports and opportunities.

Early Signs and Symptoms

Autism spectrum disorder (ASD) is a developmental disorder that affects social interaction, communication, and behavior. It is typically diagnosed in early childhood and can have a significant impact on a person's life. While the exact causes of autism are still not fully understood, researchers have identified some early signs and symptoms that can help with early detection and intervention.

One of the earliest signs of autism is a lack of or delay in language development. Children with autism may not begin speaking at the typical age or may not use language in the same way as other children. For example, they may repeat words or phrases over and over, or use language in a very literal way. They may also have difficulty understanding and responding to verbal and nonverbal communication from others.

Another early sign of autism is a lack of interest in social interaction. Children with autism may seem uninterested in playing with other children or may have difficulty understanding social cues and norms. They may also have difficulty making eye contact, using gestures, or responding appropriately to the emotions of others.

Repetitive behaviors and routines are also common in children with autism. They may have strict routines and rituals that they need to follow or become very upset if these routines are disrupted. They may also engage in repetitive behaviors, such as hand-flapping or lining up toys, that serve no apparent purpose.

Sensory sensitivities are another common feature of autism. Children with autism may be hypersensitive or hyposensitive to certain stimuli, such as noise, light, or touch. They may become overwhelmed or distressed by certain sensory experiences or seek out certain sensory experiences to the exclusion of others.

It is important to note that not all children with autism will exhibit all of these early signs and symptoms, and that some children with autism may not show any signs until later in childhood. However, early detection and intervention can make a significant difference in the long-term outcomes for children with autism.

If you suspect that your child may have autism, it is important to speak with your pediatrician or a qualified healthcare provider. They can help evaluate your child's development and refer you to specialists for further evaluation and support.

In addition, there are many resources available for parents and caregivers of children with autism. Autism advocacy organizations, such as the Autism Society and Autism Speaks, provide information, support, and resources for families affected by autism. There are also many therapy and educational interventions available that can help children with autism develop social and communication skills, manage sensory sensitivities, and improve their overall quality of life.

Causes and Risk Factors

Autism spectrum disorder (ASD) is a complex neurodevelopmental condition that affects social communication and behavior. It is believed that both genetic and environmental factors contribute to the development of ASD. Below we will explore the causes and risk factors associated with autism.

Genetic factors play a significant role in the development of autism. Studies have shown that the risk of developing autism is higher in families where one or more members have been diagnosed with the disorder. According to the Autism Society, the risk of autism is approximately 20 times higher for siblings of individuals with autism than for the general population. Additionally, certain genetic mutations and disorders, such as Fragile X syndrome and Rett syndrome, have been linked to an increased risk of developing autism.

Environmental factors, such as prenatal and perinatal complications, have also been associated with an increased risk of autism. Prenatal complications, such as exposure to toxins, infections, and maternal stress, have been linked to an increased risk of autism. For example, research has shown that exposure to valproic acid, a medication used to treat epilepsy and bipolar disorder, during pregnancy increases the risk of autism in offspring.

Perinatal complications, such as premature birth and low birth weight, have also been associated with an increased risk of autism. Studies have shown that children who are born prematurely are more likely to develop autism than those who are born at full term. Additionally, maternal health during pregnancy, such as gestational diabetes and obesity, has been linked to an increased risk of autism in offspring.

In addition to genetic and environmental factors, there are also other risk factors associated with autism. For example, boys are four times more likely than girls to be diagnosed with autism. The reason for this gender difference is not fully understood but may be related to hormonal and/or genetic factors.

Finally, it is important to note that there is no evidence to support the claim that vaccines cause autism. This claim originated from a 1998 study that has since been thoroughly discredited and retracted by the journal in which it was published. Numerous studies have shown that there is no causal link between vaccines and autism.

Diagnosing Autism: The Evaluation Process

Autism Spectrum Disorder (ASD) is a complex neurodevelopmental disorder that affects communication, social interaction, and behavior. Diagnosing autism can be challenging, as there are no medical tests that can definitively diagnose it. Instead, the process involves a thorough evaluation of the individual's behavior and development.

The evaluation process for diagnosing autism typically involves a team of healthcare professionals, including a pediatrician, a psychologist, and a speech and language therapist. The evaluation process may also include specialists in genetics, neurology, and psychiatry, depending on the individual's symptoms and medical history.

The evaluation typically begins with a comprehensive medical examination, including a review of the individual's developmental history and any medical conditions that may be related to autism. The healthcare professional will also ask about the individual's behavior and development, as well as their social interactions and communication skills.

Observation is an important part of the evaluation process. The healthcare professional will observe the individual's behavior and communication in different settings, such as at home, at school, and during play. They may also use standardized tests to assess the individual's cognitive, communication, and social skills.

A diagnostic interview is also typically conducted as part of the evaluation process. This interview is usually conducted with the individual's parents or caregivers, and it focuses on the individual's behavior, communication, and development.

In some cases, the evaluation may include genetic testing or a brain imaging study, such as magnetic resonance imaging (MRI) or computed tomography (CT) scan. These tests can help rule out other medical conditions that may be related to autism.

The evaluation process can be lengthy and may require multiple visits to healthcare professionals. It is important to be patient and to work closely with the healthcare team to ensure an accurate diagnosis.

It is also important to note that autism is a spectrum disorder, and individuals with autism can have a wide range of symptoms and abilities. The diagnostic criteria for autism have changed over time, and the diagnosis may not always be clear-cut.

In recent years, there has been an increased focus on early detection and intervention for autism. Early intervention can improve outcomes and help individuals with autism reach their full potential. If you suspect that your child may have autism, it is important to speak with your healthcare provider as soon as possible.

Chapter Two

Autism Spectrum Disorder Types

Autism Spectrum Disorder (ASD) is a complex developmental disorder that affects social interaction, communication, and behavior. According to the Centers for Disease Control and Prevention (CDC), about one in 54 children in the United States has been diagnosed with ASD. However, not all individuals with ASD present the same symptoms, and there are several types of ASD that can be differentiated based on their characteristics.

The diagnostic criteria for ASD underwent significant changes in 2013 with the publication of the fifth edition of the Diagnostic and Statistical Manual of Mental Disorders (DSM-5). The DSM-5 replaced the previous diagnostic categories of Autistic Disorder, Asperger's Disorder, and Pervasive Developmental Disorder Not Otherwise Specified (PDD-NOS) with the single diagnosis of ASD, which includes different levels of severity based on the presence of social communication deficits and restricted, repetitive behaviors and interests.

One way to differentiate the types of ASD is by their severity levels, which are defined based on the level of support the individual requires to function in daily life. The severity levels are:

1. Level 1: Requiring support

Individuals with Level 1 ASD, also known as mild ASD, require some support to function in social situations. They may have difficulty initiating or responding to social interactions, and may engage in repetitive behaviors or have narrow interests. However, they can usually function independently in daily life.

2. Level 2: Requiring substantial support

Individuals with Level 2 ASD, also known as moderate ASD, require substantial support to function in social situations. They may have more pronounced social communication deficits, and may engage in more repetitive behaviors or have more narrow interests. They may also require some support with daily living tasks.

3. Level 3: Requiring very substantial support

Individuals with Level 3 ASD, also known as severe ASD, require very substantial support to function in social situations. They may have very limited social communication skills and may engage in intense and frequent repetitive behaviors or have very narrow interests. They typically require significant support with daily living tasks.

Another way to differentiate types of ASD is by the presence of certain features or associated conditions. Some types of ASD based on these features or conditions are:

Asperger's Syndrome

Asperger's Syndrome is no longer a separate diagnosis under the DSM-5, but some individuals previously diagnosed with Asperger's may now be diagnosed with Level 1 ASD. Individuals with Asperger's typically have normal intelligence and language skills, but have difficulty with social communication and may engage in repetitive behaviors or have narrow interests.

Rett Syndrome

Rett Syndrome is a rare genetic disorder that almost exclusively affects females. Individuals with Rett Syndrome typically experience a regression in skills after a period of normal development, and may have severe communication and motor impairments.

Childhood Disintegrative Disorder

Childhood Disintegrative Disorder is a rare condition in which children develop normally until around the age of two, but then experience a significant regression in skills, including social communication, language, and motor abilities.

Fragile X Syndrome

Fragile X Syndrome is a genetic condition that affects both males and females. Individuals with Fragile X Syndrome typically have intellectual disabilities, and may also have social communication deficits and repetitive behaviors.

It is important to note that while these types of ASD are distinct in their features and associated conditions, there is significant overlap between them, and not all individuals with ASD fit neatly into one category. Additionally, individuals with ASD may have co-occurring conditions such as anxiety, depression, or attention deficit hyperactivity disorder (ADHD), which can further complicate diagnosis and treatment.

Asperger's Syndrome

Asperger's syndrome is a type of autism spectrum disorder (ASD) that affects how individuals perceive and socialize with others. It was first described by Austrian pediatrician Hans Asperger in 1944. Below we will discuss Asperger's syndrome, including its symptoms, causes, diagnosis, and treatment.

Symptoms of Asperger's syndrome vary widely between individuals, but there are some common signs. Individuals with Asperger's may have difficulty with social interactions, such as making eye contact or understanding social cues like body language or tone of voice. They may also struggle with making friends and may seem socially awkward or inappropriate. Another common symptom is a strong focus on one topic or interest, which can be intense and all-consuming. This intense focus can make it difficult for them to engage in other activities or switch to different topics of conversation.

Other symptoms of Asperger's syndrome may include repetitive behaviors, rigid routines, sensitivity to sensory input such as certain sounds or textures, and difficulty with nonverbal communication. It is important to note that these symptoms can vary in severity and can affect individuals differently.

The exact cause of Asperger's syndrome is not known, but it is believed to be a combination of genetic and environmental factors. Some studies suggest that the disorder may be caused by abnormalities in the structure and function of the brain. Research has also shown that certain genes may increase the risk of developing Asperger's syndrome.

Diagnosing Asperger's syndrome can be challenging because there is no specific test to confirm the disorder. Instead, doctors and mental health professionals rely on a comprehensive evaluation that includes observing behavior and developmental history, as well as conducting interviews with family members and caregivers. This evaluation may also include standardized tests and assessments to evaluate cognitive and social functioning.

Treatment for Asperger's syndrome typically involves a combination of therapies, including behavioral and educational interventions, medications, and support services. Behavioral and educational interventions may include social skills training, cognitive-behavioral therapy, and speech and language therapy. Medications may be used to manage symptoms such as anxiety or depression, while support services may include individual or group therapy, counseling, and vocational training.

Rett Syndrome

Rett Syndrome is a rare neurodevelopmental disorder that primarily affects girls, with an estimated incidence of 1 in 10,000 to 15,000 females born. It is a genetic disorder caused by mutations in the MECP2 gene, which provides instructions for producing a protein called methyl-CpG-binding protein 2. This protein plays a crucial role in the development and function of nerve cells in the brain. Mutations in the MECP2 gene lead to a deficiency or dysfunction of the protein, resulting in the characteristic symptoms of Rett Syndrome.

The symptoms of Rett Syndrome usually become apparent between 6 and 18 months of age, as the child's development starts to regress. The child may lose previously acquired language and motor skills, such as the ability to speak, crawl, or walk. Other symptoms may include repetitive hand movements, such as wringing or clapping, breathing difficulties, seizures, abnormal muscle tone, and scoliosis.

There are four stages of Rett Syndrome, which are usually progressive but may vary in severity and duration for each individual. The first stage is called the early onset or stagnation stage, which usually lasts for several months to a year. During this stage, the child may experience a slowing of head growth and a loss of interest in toys or social interaction.

The second stage is called the rapid destructive stage, which usually lasts for several months to a year. During this stage, the child may experience a significant loss of language and motor skills, as well as the development of stereotypic hand movements and breathing irregularities.

The third stage is called the plateau stage, which usually lasts for several years. During this stage, the child's condition stabilizes, and there may be some improvement in communication and motor skills.

The fourth and final stage is called the late motor deterioration stage, which usually occurs in adolescence or early adulthood. During this stage, the individual may experience a loss of mobility, scoliosis, and other physical complications.

There is currently no cure for Rett Syndrome, and treatment is mainly supportive and focused on managing symptoms. Treatment may include medication for seizures, respiratory support, physical therapy, and behavioral therapy. Research is ongoing, and several clinical trials are currently underway to investigate potential therapies for Rett Syndrome.

Childhood Disintegrative Disorder

Childhood Disintegrative Disorder (CDD) is a rare and severe developmental disorder that affects children. Also known as Heller's syndrome or disintegrative psychosis, it is a type of autism spectrum disorder (ASD) that typically occurs in early childhood. This disorder is characterized by a significant loss of previously acquired social, communication, and cognitive skills. Below we will provide an overview of CDD, including its symptoms, causes, and treatment options.

Symptoms:

Children with CDD typically develop normally in the first two to four years of life, after which they start to lose previously acquired skills such as language, social interaction, and play skills. Some of the symptoms of CDD include:

1. Loss of language skills: Children with CDD may stop using words or phrases that they previously learned, or they may develop difficulty in forming sentences.

2. Loss of social skills: They may have trouble with social interactions and fail to engage in age-appropriate play with other children.

3. Repetitive behaviors: Like other autism spectrum disorders, CDD is also associated with repetitive behaviors such as hand flapping, rocking, or spinning.

4. Loss of cognitive skills: Children with CDD may experience a significant decline in cognitive abilities such as memory, problem-solving, and attention span.

5. Loss of bowel and bladder control: Children with CDD may have difficulty controlling their bowel and bladder functions.

Causes:

The exact cause of CDD is unknown. However, research suggests that it may be caused by a combination of genetic and environmental factors. Some studies have found a link between CDD and abnormalities in the brain's structure and function. Other studies have suggested that the disorder may be caused by a genetic mutation that affects the development of the brain.

Treatment:

Currently, there is no cure for CDD. Treatment focuses on managing the symptoms and improving the child's quality of life. Some of the treatment options for CDD include:

6. Medications: Medications such as antipsychotics and antidepressants can help manage some of the symptoms of CDD, such as anxiety and aggression.

7. Behavioral therapy: Behavioral therapy such as Applied Behavioral Analysis (ABA) can help children with CDD learn new skills and behaviors.

8. Speech therapy: Speech therapy can help children with CDD improve their language skills.

9. Occupational therapy: Occupational therapy can help children with CDD develop fine motor skills and improve their ability to perform daily activities.

10. Educational support: Children with CDD may benefit from special education programs that are designed to meet their unique needs.

Pervasive Developmental Disorder-Not Otherwise Specified (PDD-NOS)

Pervasive Developmental Disorder-Not Otherwise Specified (PDD-NOS) is a term used to describe a wide range of developmental disorders that are not classified as Autism Spectrum Disorders (ASD) or other specific developmental disorders. It is considered to be a subtype of ASD, but with less specific symptoms and characteristics.

PDD-NOS is a diagnosis that is given when a child or adult shows some, but not all, of the symptoms of ASD. This can be confusing for parents and caregivers, as it can be difficult to understand why their child is not classified as having full-blown autism, but still has some significant developmental challenges.

Symptoms of PDD-NOS can vary widely depending on the individual, but typically involve difficulty with social interactions and communication skills, as well as repetitive behaviors and interests. These symptoms can range from mild to severe, and may be more or less noticeable in different situations.

Some common symptoms of PDD-NOS may include difficulty with social skills, such as making eye contact, understanding social cues, and interacting with others in a typical way. Communication difficulties may include delayed speech or language development, and difficulty understanding or using language appropriately.

Individuals with PDD-NOS may also have repetitive behaviors or interests, such as a strong focus on a specific topic or object, or the need for a structured routine or schedule. They may have difficulty with changes in routine or new situations, and may become upset or agitated when faced with unfamiliar or unpredictable situations.

Diagnosing PDD-NOS can be challenging, as there is no one specific test or diagnostic criteria. Instead, a diagnosis is typically made based on a combination of clinical observations, developmental assessments, and standardized diagnostic tools.

Treatment for PDD-NOS typically involves a combination of therapies and interventions aimed at addressing specific symptoms and challenges. These may include speech and language therapy, occupational therapy, behavior therapy, and social skills training.

One of the challenges of treating PDD-NOS is that the symptoms can be quite varied and may affect different areas of development in different ways. As such, treatment plans are often tailored to the individual needs of each patient, with a focus on addressing the specific challenges and symptoms that are most problematic.

In many cases, early intervention and treatment can be very effective in helping individuals with PDD-NOS to improve their social and communication skills, and to develop strategies for coping with their symptoms and challenges. However, ongoing support and intervention may be necessary throughout childhood and into adulthood in order to help individuals with PDD-NOS achieve their full potential.

Chapter Three

Autism and Development

Autism is a developmental disorder that affects a person's ability to communicate, socialize, and interact with the world around them. The condition is characterized by repetitive behaviors, restricted interests, and difficulty with social communication and interaction. Autism is typically diagnosed in early childhood, and while there is no cure, early intervention and therapy can greatly improve outcomes for individuals with autism.

Developmental delays are often the first signs of autism. Infants with autism may not respond to their name or may avoid eye contact with others. They may not engage in social interaction with others, such as playing peek-a-boo or pointing at objects to show interest. As they get older, children with autism may struggle to make friends, have difficulty with nonverbal communication, and may have trouble understanding social cues.

Language development is also affected in children with autism. Some children may develop language later than their peers or may have difficulty with expressive language. They may also have trouble understanding non-literal language, such as jokes or sarcasm.

Motor development is also affected in some children with autism. They may have difficulty with coordination, balance, and fine motor skills, such as holding a pencil or buttoning their shirt. Some children with autism may engage in repetitive behaviors, such as hand-flapping or rocking back and forth.

Autism is a spectrum disorder, meaning that the severity of symptoms can vary widely from person to person. Some individuals may have mild symptoms and be able to live independently, while others may have more severe symptoms that require lifelong support and care.

There are many factors that can contribute to the development of autism, including genetic and environmental factors. While there is no single cause of autism, research has shown that genetics play a significant role in the development of the disorder. Environmental factors, such as exposure to toxins during pregnancy or complications during birth, may also contribute to the development of autism.

Early intervention and therapy are crucial for individuals with autism. Early diagnosis and treatment can help children develop social, communication, and cognitive skills that will improve their ability to function independently. Applied Behavior Analysis (ABA) therapy is a common type of therapy used to help children with autism learn new skills and behaviors. Speech therapy, occupational therapy, and sensory integration therapy are also commonly used to help children with autism.

In addition to therapy, parents and caregivers can also support children with autism by creating a structured and predictable environment. This can include establishing routines for daily activities, such as meals and bedtime, and providing visual schedules to help children understand what is expected of them. It is also important to provide plenty of opportunities for social interaction and play.

While autism is a lifelong condition, with the right support and treatment, individuals with autism can live happy and fulfilling lives. By understanding the signs and symptoms of autism and seeking early intervention and therapy, parents and caregivers can help children with autism develop the skills and abilities they need to reach their full potential.

Communication Skills and Challenges

Communication is a vital part of human interaction and helps us to form relationships and connect with one another. For individuals with Autism Spectrum Disorder (ASD), communication can be a significant challenge. ASD is a neurodevelopmental disorder that affects communication and social interaction, and often includes restricted, repetitive behaviors or interests. Below we will explore communication skills and challenges for individuals with ASD.

Communication is a broad term that encompasses various aspects of social interaction, including verbal and nonverbal communication, such as facial expressions, body language, eye contact, and tone of voice. For individuals with ASD, communication challenges can be significant, as they may have difficulty with social communication and understanding nonverbal cues.

One of the most significant challenges for individuals with ASD is in the area of social communication, which includes the use of language for social purposes, such as greeting others, initiating and maintaining conversations, and responding appropriately to others. Individuals with ASD may have difficulty with understanding the social context of conversations and may struggle to use language effectively to communicate their thoughts, feelings, and needs.

Another challenge for individuals with ASD is in understanding nonverbal cues, such as facial expressions, body language, and tone of voice. These cues play an essential role in social communication and can help individuals to understand the emotions and intentions of others. However, individuals with ASD may have difficulty interpreting and using these cues effectively, leading to miscommunication and misunderstandings.

Additionally, individuals with ASD may have difficulty with pragmatics, which refers to the social rules and conventions of language. Pragmatics involves understanding the appropriate use of language in different social situations, such as formal vs. informal language, polite vs. impolite language, and the use of humor and sarcasm. Individuals with ASD may struggle with these social rules and conventions, which can make communication more challenging.

Despite these challenges, many individuals with ASD do have the ability to communicate effectively. However, they may need support and intervention to develop and improve their communication skills. Speech and language therapy is a common intervention for individuals with ASD, which focuses on developing language and social communication skills, as well as improving pragmatic language abilities.

In addition to speech and language therapy, there are several strategies that can be used to support communication for individuals with ASD. These include using visual aids, such as pictures, symbols, and social stories, to help individuals understand social situations and communicate effectively. Augmentative and alternative communication (AAC) devices, such as tablets or picture boards, can also be used to support communication for individuals with limited verbal abilities.

Another strategy for supporting communication in individuals with ASD is to use a structured approach to social communication. This involves breaking down social situations into smaller, more manageable steps and teaching individuals with ASD how to navigate these steps effectively. For example, teaching individuals with ASD how to initiate a conversation, maintain eye contact, and respond appropriately to others.

Social Skills and Interaction

Social interaction and communication are crucial parts of human behavior, which can be challenging for individuals with autism. Autism spectrum disorder (ASD) is a neurodevelopmental disorder that affects an individual's social interaction, communication, and behavior. The way people with autism interact socially differs from the norm, making it challenging for them to understand social cues and nonverbal communication.

Social skills and interaction are two areas where individuals with autism often struggle. While some individuals with autism may be talkative, they may not understand how to initiate or maintain a conversation or read nonverbal cues. Others may prefer to be alone and may struggle to engage in social interaction altogether.

One of the core symptoms of autism is social communication difficulties. Individuals with autism may have a difficult time initiating and maintaining conversations, understanding sarcasm or jokes, taking turns in conversations, and following social cues. They may also struggle to understand social rules, which can lead to misinterpretation of social situations and inappropriate responses.

Another issue that people with autism may face is difficulty with social reciprocity. Social reciprocity involves sharing interests, maintaining eye contact, taking turns, and initiating interactions. Children with autism may struggle with these skills, leading to difficulties in making and maintaining friendships.

Some individuals with autism may also have difficulty with understanding emotions and facial expressions. They may have trouble recognizing and interpreting the emotions of others, making it difficult to form meaningful relationships. They may also struggle with displaying appropriate emotions in response to a situation, leading to inappropriate or unexpected emotional responses.

However, it is important to note that the severity of social interaction and communication challenges can vary greatly among individuals with autism. While some individuals may have difficulty with these skills, others may have relatively strong social and communication skills.

Early intervention is crucial in helping individuals with autism develop their social skills and interact more effectively with others. Programs such as social skills training, speech therapy, and occupational therapy can help individuals with autism improve their communication and social interaction skills. They can also learn how to recognize and interpret social cues and understand social rules.

Additionally, parents and caregivers can play an essential role in helping children with autism develop social skills. They can provide opportunities for children to engage in social activities, such as play dates or community events. Parents can also work with therapists to develop strategies and techniques to help children improve their social interaction and communication skills.

Behavioral Patterns and Repetitive Behaviors

Autism is a developmental disorder that affects an individual's behavior, communication, and social interactions. One of the most common features of autism is the presence of repetitive behaviors or interests. These behaviors may manifest as a particular routine, an attachment to specific objects, or other repetitive actions. Understanding these behaviors and finding ways to manage them can help individuals with autism to improve their quality of life.

Repetitive behaviors are often seen as a way for individuals with autism to cope with their environment. They can provide a sense of familiarity and control in an otherwise overwhelming and unpredictable world. These behaviors can also serve as a way to communicate needs or desires when verbal communication is difficult.

There are several different types of repetitive behaviors commonly associated with autism. These include:

1. Stereotypy: This involves repetitive body movements, such as rocking back and forth, flapping hands, or spinning in circles.

2. Rituals: This refers to the need for routine and predictability, often demonstrated through a specific order of actions or rituals that must be followed.

3. Fixations: This involves an intense interest in a particular object or topic, which may dominate an individual's thoughts and behaviors.

4. Sensory behaviors: These may include behaviors such as rubbing surfaces or textures, seeking out certain sounds or smells, or avoiding certain sensations.

5. Self-injurious behaviors: This refers to behaviors that can cause harm to oneself, such as head-banging or biting.

These behaviors can have a significant impact on an individual's daily life, as well as the lives of their family members and caregivers. However, with appropriate support and interventions, many individuals with autism can learn to manage these behaviors and develop more adaptive coping strategies.

One effective approach to managing repetitive behaviors is through the use of behavioral therapy. Applied Behavioral Analysis (ABA) is a type of therapy that focuses on teaching new skills and behaviors, and has been shown to be effective in reducing repetitive behaviors in individuals with autism. This therapy uses positive reinforcement to encourage desirable behaviors, and may involve breaking down complex behaviors into smaller, more manageable steps.

Other interventions that may be helpful in managing repetitive behaviors include:

6. Sensory integration therapy: This therapy focuses on addressing sensory processing difficulties that may underlie certain repetitive behaviors.

7. Cognitive behavioral therapy: This type of therapy can help individuals with autism to identify and challenge negative thought patterns and develop more adaptive coping strategies.

8. Medications: Certain medications, such as selective serotonin reuptake inhibitors (SSRIs), may be effective in reducing repetitive behaviors in some individuals with autism.

In addition to these interventions, it is important to create a supportive environment that minimizes stress and maximizes predictability. This can involve creating a consistent daily routine, providing clear and concise instructions, and avoiding situations that may trigger anxiety or overstimulation.

Sensory Processing Issues

Sensory processing issues are a common feature of Autism Spectrum Disorder (ASD) and can cause significant challenges for individuals with the condition. Sensory processing issues refer to difficulties in receiving and interpreting sensory information, such as touch, smell, sound, taste, and sight. These challenges can lead to oversensitivity or undersensitivity to sensory input, causing discomfort, anxiety, and other behavioral issues.

Sensory processing issues are caused by differences in the way the brain of an individual with ASD processes sensory information. The brain may overreact to certain stimuli or not react enough, leading to a sensory overload or underload. This can result in difficulties with daily activities, social interaction, and learning.

One common sensory processing issue in individuals with ASD is hypersensitivity or oversensitivity to sensory input. This can manifest in a variety of ways, including sensitivity to bright lights or loud sounds, discomfort with certain textures or fabrics, and aversion to strong smells. Individuals with hypersensitivity may find it challenging to participate in everyday activities, such as going to school, attending social events, or traveling on public transportation.

On the other hand, some individuals with ASD may experience hyposensitivity or undersensitivity to sensory input. They may have difficulty feeling pain or recognizing when they are hungry, thirsty, or need to use the restroom. This can lead to health and safety issues, as well as difficulties with self-care.

Sensory processing issues can also cause difficulties with social interaction. Individuals with hypersensitivity may become overwhelmed in social situations or avoid them altogether, leading to isolation and loneliness. Those with hyposensitivity may have difficulty recognizing social cues, making it challenging to communicate effectively with others.

Repetitive behaviors, another common feature of ASD, can also be related to sensory processing issues. Some individuals may engage in repetitive behaviors, such as hand flapping or rocking, as a way to self-soothe or regulate sensory input.

Fortunately, there are strategies and interventions that can help individuals with sensory processing issues. Occupational therapy can be particularly helpful in addressing sensory challenges, as it focuses on improving everyday functioning through the use of sensory integration techniques.

One intervention used in occupational therapy is the use of sensory diets. Sensory diets are personalized plans that provide individuals with specific sensory input throughout the day to help regulate their sensory system. For example, an individual with hypersensitivity to touch may benefit from using a weighted blanket or participating in activities that provide deep pressure, such as swimming or bouncing on a therapy ball.

Another intervention is the use of visual supports, such as picture schedules, to help individuals with ASD prepare for sensory experiences. This can help reduce anxiety and prepare them for upcoming events, such as a loud concert or a busy public place.

It is essential to note that sensory processing issues are not unique to ASD and can be present in individuals without the condition. However, sensory challenges can be particularly significant for individuals with ASD and can contribute to challenges with social interaction, communication, and behavior.

Chapter Four

Therapies and Interventions

Therapies and interventions can be crucial in helping individuals with autism spectrum disorder (ASD) develop social and communication skills, manage behaviors and sensory issues, and improve overall quality of life. There is no single therapy or intervention that works for everyone with ASD, and treatment plans are typically tailored to each individual's unique needs and strengths. Below we will discuss various therapies and interventions commonly used in the treatment of ASD.

Applied Behavior Analysis (ABA) is a therapy that is widely used to treat ASD. ABA is based on the principle that positive reinforcement can be used to increase desired behaviors and decrease undesired behaviors. ABA therapy is typically intensive, with several hours of one-on-one therapy sessions each week, and may involve a range of techniques, including verbal prompts, positive reinforcement, and modeling.

Occupational therapy is another therapy that can be beneficial for individuals with ASD. Occupational therapists work with individuals to develop skills necessary for everyday life, such as self-care, socialization, and communication. This may involve developing strategies for sensory processing issues, teaching social skills, and developing motor skills.

Speech therapy is often used to help individuals with ASD develop communication skills. This may include working on speech articulation, developing nonverbal communication skills, and teaching language comprehension. Speech therapy can also help individuals with ASD learn how to use social communication skills in everyday situations.

Physical therapy can also be beneficial for individuals with ASD. This type of therapy focuses on developing physical skills and improving overall motor function. Physical therapists may work with individuals with ASD to develop strength, coordination, balance, and flexibility.

In addition to these therapies, there are several other interventions that can be beneficial for individuals with ASD. These include:

1. Social skills groups: These groups are designed to help individuals with ASD develop social skills, such as communication, empathy, and understanding social cues.

2. Cognitive-behavioral therapy (CBT): This therapy is often used to help individuals with ASD manage anxiety and other emotional and behavioral issues.

3. Medication: While medication is not a cure for ASD, certain medications can be used to manage symptoms such as anxiety, depression, and hyperactivity.

4. Assistive technology: This includes devices such as communication boards, tablets, and other tools that can help individuals with ASD communicate more effectively.

5. Parent training and support: Parents of children with ASD often benefit from training and support to help them better understand their child's needs and how to support their child's development.

It is important to note that there is no single "cure" for ASD, and therapies and interventions must be tailored to each individual's unique needs and strengths. It may take time and patience to find the right combination of therapies and interventions for an individual with ASD, but with proper support and treatment, individuals with ASD can lead fulfilling and meaningful lives.

Applied Behavior Analysis (ABA)

Applied Behavior Analysis (ABA) is a widely recognized therapy for individuals with Autism Spectrum Disorder (ASD) and has been shown to be effective in improving social, communication, and behavioral skills in individuals with ASD. Below we will discuss what ABA is, how it works, and its benefits for individuals with ASD.

ABA is a behavioral therapy that focuses on modifying behaviors in order to improve a person's quality of life. It is based on the principles of behaviorism, which emphasize the role of the environment in shaping behavior. ABA therapy involves breaking down complex behaviors into smaller, more manageable components and teaching new behaviors through a process called behavior shaping.

Behavior shaping involves breaking down a desired behavior into small, achievable steps and reinforcing each step along the way. This reinforcement can take the form of praise, rewards, or other positive feedback. ABA also involves using positive reinforcement to reduce unwanted behaviors, such as tantrums or self-injury.

One of the key components of ABA is the use of data collection and analysis. ABA therapists collect data on a child's behavior and use this data to track progress and make decisions about what skills to target next. This data-driven approach allows therapists to tailor the therapy to the individual needs of the child and make adjustments as necessary.

ABA can be implemented in a variety of settings, including home, school, and clinic settings. It typically involves one-on-one sessions between the therapist and the child, although group sessions may also be used. ABA therapy is often intensive, with sessions occurring multiple times per week and lasting for several hours at a time.

There are many benefits of ABA therapy for individuals with ASD. One of the most significant benefits is the improvement in social and communication skills. ABA therapy can help children learn to communicate effectively, make eye contact, and engage in social interactions with others.

ABA can also help individuals with ASD learn new skills and reduce unwanted behaviors. For example, ABA therapy can be used to teach daily living skills, such as dressing and grooming, as well as academic skills, such as reading and math. ABA therapy can also help reduce repetitive or self-injurious behaviors, such as hand-flapping or head-banging.

In addition to these benefits, ABA therapy has also been shown to have long-lasting effects. Many children who receive ABA therapy continue to make progress and improve their skills even after the therapy has ended.

While ABA therapy has many benefits, it is important to note that it is not a cure for ASD. It is a tool that can be used to help individuals with ASD improve their skills and behaviors, but it is not a replacement for other therapies or treatments.

Occupational Therapy

Occupational therapy (OT) is a type of therapy that aims to help individuals perform daily activities and tasks more effectively and independently. OT is often used as a treatment approach for individuals with autism spectrum disorder (ASD). Autism is a neurodevelopmental disorder that affects social interaction, communication, and behavior. People with autism have difficulty processing sensory information, which can impact their ability to function in daily life. Occupational therapy is a vital part of the treatment plan for many individuals with autism.

Occupational therapy for individuals with autism involves the use of functional activities to help individuals learn new skills or improve their current abilities. Occupational therapists assess an individual's strengths and weaknesses and work with them to develop a plan that focuses on improving their ability to participate in daily activities. This may include working on skills such as dressing, grooming, and feeding oneself. It can also include working on social skills, such as communication and interpersonal relationships. Occupational therapists may also work with individuals to develop sensory integration techniques to help them process sensory information more effectively.

One of the primary goals of occupational therapy for individuals with autism is to promote independence and improve quality of life. OT sessions are typically structured and goal-oriented, with a focus on developing skills that are applicable to daily life. OT sessions may include activities such as playing with toys, doing puzzles, or practicing social skills in a group setting. The activities are designed to be fun and engaging while also promoting skill development.

Another important aspect of occupational therapy for individuals with autism is the use of visual supports. Many individuals with autism have difficulty understanding verbal instructions or processing information presented in a traditional classroom setting. Visual supports can help individuals better understand instructions and communicate their needs. These visual supports may include picture schedules, social stories, or visual cues.

Occupational therapy can also be helpful in addressing sensory issues in individuals with autism. Sensory integration therapy is a type of occupational therapy that is designed to help individuals with autism process sensory information more effectively. This may involve activities such as swinging, bouncing, or playing with tactile materials to help the individual become more comfortable with different sensory inputs.

Occupational therapy can also help individuals with autism develop fine motor skills, such as writing or cutting with scissors. Developing these skills can be particularly important for school-aged children with autism, as it can help them succeed in academic settings.

In addition to traditional occupational therapy sessions, occupational therapists may also work with individuals with autism in their home or school environments. This can help the individual develop skills in real-world settings and promote generalization of skills learned in therapy to daily life.

Speech and Language Therapy

Autism spectrum disorder (ASD) is a neurodevelopmental condition that affects communication, social interaction, and behavior. One of the hallmark characteristics of ASD is difficulty with communication, including verbal and nonverbal language. This can lead to challenges in making friends, participating in social activities, and succeeding in school or work. Speech and language therapy (SLT) is a common intervention used to address these communication difficulties in individuals with ASD.

SLT for ASD focuses on improving communication skills, such as expressive language (the ability to communicate one's own thoughts and ideas), receptive language (the ability to understand and interpret what others are saying), and social communication (the ability to use language in social situations). SLT may also address issues with speech production, such as articulation (pronouncing sounds and words clearly) and fluency (speaking without stuttering or hesitating).

SLT for ASD typically involves a combination of individual therapy sessions and group therapy. In individual therapy, the speech-language pathologist (SLP) works one-on-one with the individual with ASD to address their specific communication challenges. In group therapy, the SLP may work with a small group of individuals with ASD to practice social communication skills and interact with peers.

One common approach used in SLT for ASD is augmentative and alternative communication (AAC). AAC refers to any method of communication that supplements or replaces speech. This may include using visual aids such as picture symbols or communication boards, or high-tech devices such as speech-generating devices or computer software. AAC can be especially helpful for individuals with ASD who have limited verbal communication abilities.

Another approach used in SLT for ASD is social communication intervention. This involves teaching individuals with ASD social communication skills, such as making eye contact, taking turns in conversation, and interpreting nonverbal cues. Social communication intervention may also involve teaching individuals with ASD how to initiate and maintain friendships, engage in group activities, and navigate social situations.

SLT for ASD may also address sensory processing issues. Many individuals with ASD have difficulty processing sensory information, such as sounds, sights, and textures. This can impact their ability to communicate and interact with others. SLT may include sensory integration therapy, which involves using sensory activities to help individuals with ASD regulate their sensory input and improve their communication and social skills.

The effectiveness of SLT for ASD varies depending on the individual's specific communication challenges and the intensity and duration of the therapy. However, research suggests that SLT can be beneficial for improving communication skills in individuals with ASD. Studies have shown that SLT can lead to improvements in expressive language, receptive language, and social communication skills. Additionally, SLT may also improve academic performance and social skills.

Social Skills Training

1. Social Skills Training for Autism: An Overview

Autism spectrum disorder (ASD) is a neurodevelopmental disorder that affects communication, behavior, and social interaction. Individuals with ASD often experience difficulties in social situations and forming relationships with others. Social skills training (SST) is an intervention that aims to help individuals with ASD develop and improve their social skills. Below we will explore the benefits and techniques of SST for individuals with ASD.

What is Social Skills Training (SST)?

SST is a type of therapy that focuses on teaching individuals social skills that they may be lacking. This type of therapy is often used for individuals with ASD who have difficulty with social interaction. The goals of SST include improving communication, increasing self-awareness, and developing social relationships. The techniques used in SST vary depending on the individual's age and level of functioning.

Benefits of SST for Autism

Research has shown that SST can be effective in improving social skills in individuals with ASD. SST has been found to improve communication skills, increase social interaction, and reduce social anxiety. SST can also improve daily living skills and reduce problematic behaviors.

One study found that children with ASD who received SST showed improvement in social interaction, communication, and overall adaptive functioning. Another study found that SST can improve social skills and adaptive behavior in adults with ASD.

Techniques Used in SST for Autism

There are several techniques used in SST for individuals with ASD, including:

2. Role-Playing: Role-playing is a technique where the individual practices social skills in a safe and controlled environment. This technique allows the individual to practice social interaction in a low-stress setting.

3. Video Modeling: Video modeling is a technique where the individual watches videos of social interactions and then imitates those interactions in real-life situations. This technique has been found to be effective in improving social skills in individuals with ASD.

4. Social Stories: Social stories are short stories that describe social situations and appropriate behavior. Social stories can help individuals with ASD understand social situations and develop appropriate social skills.

5. Peer-Mediated Instruction and Intervention (PMII): PMII is a technique where peers are trained to provide social support and feedback to individuals with ASD. PMII has been found to be effective in improving social skills in children with ASD.

6. Cognitive-Behavioral Therapy (CBT): CBT is a type of therapy that focuses on changing negative thought patterns and behaviors. CBT can be

effective in reducing social anxiety and improving social skills in individuals with ASD.

Chapter Five

Navigating the Educational System

Navigating the Educational System with Autism

Autism Spectrum Disorder (ASD) affects many aspects of an individual's life, including education. The educational system can be complex and overwhelming for individuals with ASD and their families. However, with the right support and knowledge, individuals with ASD can succeed in the educational system.

Below we will explore how individuals with ASD can navigate the educational system successfully. We will discuss the importance of early intervention, the roles of educators and parents, and the legal protections available to individuals with ASD.

Early Intervention

Early intervention is crucial for individuals with ASD to succeed in the educational system. Early intervention refers to any support or therapy given to individuals with ASD before they enter school. Early intervention is important because it helps to identify and address the developmental delays and difficulties associated with ASD at an early age.

Early intervention can involve a range of therapies, including Applied Behavior Analysis (ABA), speech therapy, and occupational therapy. These therapies can help individuals with ASD develop communication skills, social skills, and self-regulation skills.

It is important to note that early intervention is not limited to therapies. Early intervention can also involve developing individualized education plans (IEPs) and 504 plans to support individuals with ASD in the school environment. These plans can include accommodations such as preferential seating, extra time for assignments, and access to assistive technology.

Role of Educators

Educators play a vital role in the educational success of individuals with ASD. It is important for educators to have a thorough understanding of ASD and its impact on learning. Educators can work with families and support teams to develop individualized plans that meet the needs of the student.

In addition, educators can create a supportive learning environment by implementing strategies such as visual supports, sensory breaks, and social stories. Visual supports can help individuals with ASD understand expectations and routines, while sensory breaks can help individuals regulate their sensory input. Social stories can help individuals with ASD understand social situations and appropriate behavior.

It is important for educators to work closely with families and support teams to ensure consistency across settings. Consistency can help individuals with ASD feel more comfortable and confident in their environment and increase their chances of success.

Role of Parents

Parents play a critical role in supporting their child's educational success. Parents can work with educators and support teams to develop IEPs and 504 plans that meet the needs of their child. Parents can also provide valuable insight into their child's strengths, challenges, and preferences.

In addition, parents can advocate for their child's needs and ensure that their child's rights are protected. This may involve working with the school district to ensure that their child receives the appropriate accommodations and services, as well as navigating the legal system if necessary.

Legal Protections

Individuals with ASD are protected by federal and state laws, including the Individuals with Disabilities Education Act (IDEA) and Section 504 of the Rehabilitation Act of 1973. These laws require schools to provide accommodations and services to individuals with disabilities, including individuals with ASD.

IDEA requires schools to provide a free and appropriate public education (FAPE) to individuals with disabilities. This includes the provision of special education services and supports, such as IEPs, to meet the unique needs of the student.

Section 504 requires schools to provide reasonable accommodations to individuals with disabilities to ensure that they have equal access to educational opportunities. This may include accommodations such as assistive technology, preferential seating, and extra time for assignments.

In addition to federal and state laws, individuals with ASD are also protected by the Americans with Disabilities Act (ADA). The ADA prohibits discrimination against individuals with disabilities, including individuals with ASD, in all areas of public life, including education.

Individualized Education Plans (IEPs)

Individualized Education Plans (IEPs) are a crucial component in ensuring that students with autism spectrum disorder (ASD) receive the support they need to succeed in school. An IEP is a legal document that outlines the specific educational goals and accommodations that a student with a disability requires to receive a free and appropriate education.

The IEP process is initiated when a student is referred for special education services. The school district is responsible for conducting a comprehensive evaluation to determine whether the student is eligible for special education and related services. The evaluation should include a variety of assessments, such as cognitive, academic, behavioral, and adaptive functioning tests.

Once the student is determined to be eligible for special education services, a team consisting of the student's parents or guardians, teachers, school administrators, and other professionals will convene to develop the IEP. The IEP team will consider the results of the student's evaluation, as well as any information provided by the student's parents or guardians, to identify the student's strengths and weaknesses and develop appropriate educational goals.

The IEP should include specific and measurable goals that address the student's areas of need, such as communication, socialization, academics, behavior, and daily living skills. The IEP should also identify the accommodations and modifications necessary to help the student meet these goals, such as preferential seating, visual aids, communication devices, behavior plans, and extended time for assignments or testing.

It is important for parents or guardians to actively participate in the IEP process to ensure that their child's needs are being addressed. They should provide input into the development of goals and accommodations, as well as ask questions and express concerns. They should also review and sign the final IEP document to indicate their agreement or disagreement with its contents.

Once the IEP is developed, it is the school's responsibility to implement the goals and accommodations identified in the plan. The IEP team should regularly review and revise the plan as necessary to ensure that it continues to meet the student's needs.

In addition to the IEP, parents or guardians can request that their child receive additional services or supports through a 504 plan. A 504 plan is a less formal document that outlines the accommodations and modifications necessary for a student with a disability to access and participate in regular education programs and activities. While a 504 plan does not provide the same level of individualization as an IEP, it can still be a useful tool for ensuring that a student's needs are being met.

Inclusive Education and Classroom Strategies

Inclusive education is a term used to describe the practice of teaching students with disabilities, including those with autism spectrum disorder (ASD), in the same classrooms as their peers without disabilities. Inclusive education provides students with disabilities access to a high-quality education, promotes positive attitudes and friendships between students with and without disabilities, and prepares students with disabilities for post-secondary education and employment. Classroom strategies that promote inclusive education can help students with ASD to participate fully in classroom activities and improve academic and social outcomes.

One effective strategy for promoting inclusive education is the use of visual supports. Visual supports can include pictures, symbols, or written words and can help students with ASD understand classroom routines and expectations. For example, a visual schedule can help students with ASD understand the sequence of classroom activities and prepare for transitions. Visual supports can also be used to reinforce positive behavior, such as a token economy in which students earn a token for appropriate behavior that can be exchanged for a reward.

Another strategy for promoting inclusive education is peer-mediated instruction and intervention. This strategy involves training typically developing peers to provide support and assistance to students with ASD. Peer-mediated instruction and intervention can be used to promote social skills, communication, and academic skills. For example, peer-mediated instruction can involve a peer tutor working with a student with ASD to practice social skills such as turn-taking or initiating conversation. Peer-mediated intervention can involve a group of peers working together to support a student with ASD in completing a classroom project or assignment.

Universal Design for Learning (UDL) is another approach to promoting inclusive education. UDL is a framework for designing curriculum and instruction that meets the needs of all learners, including those with disabilities. UDL involves providing multiple means of representation, expression, and engagement to address the diverse learning needs of students. For example, a teacher may provide a student with ASD with multiple options for demonstrating their understanding of a concept, such as drawing a picture, writing a paragraph, or giving an oral presentation.

Collaboration between teachers, parents, and other professionals is essential to promoting inclusive education for students with ASD. Collaboration involves sharing information, working together to identify student strengths and needs, and developing and implementing effective instructional strategies. Collaboration can help to ensure that students with ASD receive the support they need to succeed in the classroom and beyond.

While inclusive education has many benefits, it is important to recognize that it may not be appropriate for all students with ASD. Some students may require more intensive services or may benefit from a specialized school setting. It is important for parents and educators to work together to determine the best educational placement for each individual student.

Transition Planning for Adolescents

Autism spectrum disorder (ASD) is a lifelong developmental disorder that affects communication, social interaction, and behavior. While the symptoms of ASD can vary widely among individuals, many people with ASD experience difficulties with transitions and changes, especially during adolescence and young adulthood. Transition planning is an important part of supporting individuals with ASD as they move from childhood to adulthood, and can help ensure that they have the necessary skills and resources to lead fulfilling and independent lives.

Transition planning for adolescents with ASD typically begins when the individual is around 14 years old and continues until they reach adulthood. The goal of transition planning is to help the individual identify their strengths, interests, and needs, and to develop a plan that will help them achieve their goals for the future. The transition planning process should involve the individual with ASD, their family, and their support team, including educators, healthcare providers, and community service providers.

One of the key components of transition planning for adolescents with ASD is developing a post-secondary education or training plan. This may involve attending college or vocational school, or participating in job training or apprenticeship programs. It is important to consider the individual's interests and abilities when developing this plan, as well as any accommodations or support they may need to be successful.

In addition to education and training, transition planning should also address employment and independent living skills. This may involve identifying potential career paths, exploring job opportunities, and developing skills such as budgeting, time management, and self-advocacy. It may also involve connecting the individual with community resources, such as housing support or vocational rehabilitation services.

Social skills and relationships are also an important part of transition planning for adolescents with ASD. This may involve developing strategies for making and maintaining friendships, as well as building skills for navigating romantic relationships. It may also involve exploring opportunities for community involvement and participation in social activities.

One of the challenges of transition planning for individuals with ASD is the variability of the disorder. While some individuals with ASD may have a strong desire for independence and may be able to manage many aspects of their lives on their own, others may require more support and guidance. It is important for transition planning to be individualized and flexible, taking into account the unique strengths and needs of each individual.

In order to be successful, transition planning for adolescents with ASD should be collaborative and involve all members of the individual's support team. This may involve regular meetings with educators, healthcare providers, and community service providers to assess progress and adjust plans as needed. It is also important to involve the individual with ASD in the planning process as much as possible, to ensure that their goals and desires are being taken into account.

Chapter Six

Family Life and Autism

Autism is a neurological disorder that affects a person's ability to communicate and interact with others. It is a complex condition that is often misunderstood by those who do not have personal experience with it. Families who have a loved one with autism face unique challenges and must learn to adapt and adjust to their situation. Below we will discuss the impact of autism on family life and the ways in which families can manage and cope with the challenges they face.

The impact of autism on family life can be profound. The condition often requires a great deal of time and attention from caregivers, and it can be emotionally and financially taxing. Families of children with autism may face additional stress due to the social isolation and lack of understanding from others. Parents may struggle with feelings of guilt, frustration, and isolation, as they try to navigate their child's diagnosis and find the best ways to support their child.

One of the most significant challenges that families of children with autism face is the cost of treatment and therapy. Many families struggle to afford the services their child needs, which can include speech therapy, occupational therapy, and behavioral therapy. Insurance coverage for these services can be limited, leaving families to pay out of pocket for treatments that can be expensive.

Another challenge that families of children with autism face is the lack of understanding from others. Many people are not familiar with the symptoms and behaviors associated with autism, and this can lead to social isolation and a lack of support. Parents may feel judged or criticized for their child's behavior, which can be hurtful and discouraging.

Despite these challenges, there are many ways in which families can manage and cope with the impact of autism on their lives. One of the most important things is to seek out support from others who understand what they are going through. This can include support groups, online forums, and other resources for families of children with autism.

Another important strategy is to stay informed about the latest research and treatment options for autism. This can help families make informed decisions about their child's care and ensure that they are accessing the most effective treatments available.

Family therapy can also be helpful in supporting families affected by autism. Therapy can help family members communicate and work together more effectively, which can help reduce stress and improve overall well-being.

Parents and caregivers of children with autism should also prioritize self-care. This can include getting enough sleep, eating a healthy diet, and finding ways to manage stress. Taking care of oneself is essential for coping with the demands of caring for a child with autism.

Parenting Strategies for Raising a Child with Autism

Parenting a child with Autism Spectrum Disorder (ASD) can present unique challenges for families. However, with the right strategies, parenting can be a fulfilling and rewarding experience. Below we will discuss some effective strategies for raising a child with ASD.

1. Educate Yourself: One of the most important things parents can do is educate themselves about ASD. This can help parents better understand their child's behaviors and needs, and provide them with the tools they need to effectively parent their child. Parents can attend workshops, read books, and consult with experts to gain a deeper understanding of ASD.

2. Create a Structured Routine: Children with ASD often thrive on routine and structure. Establishing a consistent daily routine can help reduce stress and anxiety for both the child and the parents. Consistency and predictability can also help the child feel more secure and comfortable in their environment.

3. Communicate Clearly: Children with ASD often have difficulty with communication and social interaction. As a parent, it is important to communicate in a clear and concise manner. Using visual aids, such as pictures or written instructions, can also help improve communication and reduce confusion.

4. Use Positive Reinforcement: Positive reinforcement can be a powerful tool in shaping behavior for children with ASD. Praising good behavior and rewarding positive actions can help reinforce desired behaviors and encourage children to continue them.

5. Seek Support: Raising a child with ASD can be challenging, and it is important for parents to seek support from others. This can include joining support groups, seeking counseling, and connecting with other families who have similar experiences. Support can help parents feel less isolated and better equipped to handle the challenges of parenting a child with ASD.

6. Embrace Your Child's Strengths: While children with ASD may have challenges in certain areas, they also have unique strengths and talents. As a parent, it is important to embrace and encourage your child's strengths

and interests. This can help build their confidence and sense of identity, and provide them with a sense of purpose and fulfillment.

7. Practice Self-Care: Parenting a child with ASD can be emotionally and physically draining. It is important for parents to take care of themselves, both physically and emotionally. This can include taking breaks when needed, seeking out support and resources, and engaging in activities that bring joy and relaxation.

Sibling Relationships and Autism

Autism Spectrum Disorder (ASD) can have a profound impact on family dynamics and relationships, especially between siblings. Although every family is unique, and every child with ASD is different, some common patterns and challenges may arise.

Siblings of children with ASD often experience a range of emotions, such as frustration, guilt, jealousy, and confusion. They may feel neglected or overlooked by parents who are focused on the needs of their child with autism. They may feel resentful or angry about the extra attention, resources, and time that their sibling with autism requires. They may feel embarrassed or ashamed of their sibling's unusual behavior or communication style, especially in social situations. They may feel anxious or fearful about their sibling's unpredictable outbursts, sensory sensitivities, or meltdowns.

Despite these challenges, many siblings of children with ASD also report positive experiences and attitudes. They may develop empathy, patience, and tolerance for people who are different from them. They may become advocates for autism awareness and acceptance. They may appreciate the unique strengths and talents of their sibling with autism, such as their creativity, honesty, and loyalty.

Parents can play a crucial role in fostering positive sibling relationships and addressing the challenges that may arise. Here are some parenting strategies for raising a child with autism in a way that supports their siblings as well:

1. Communication: Encourage open and honest communication among family members, and acknowledge the feelings and needs of each sibling. Provide age-appropriate information about autism and its effects, and answer questions truthfully and sensitively.

2. Quality time: Make time for each sibling individually, and provide opportunities for shared activities and interests. This can help each child feel valued and connected to their family, and can strengthen their bond with each other.

3. Support: Provide emotional support and resources for siblings, such as counseling, support groups, or educational materials. This can help them process their emotions and learn coping skills.

4. Education: Teach siblings about autism and its challenges, as well as the unique strengths and abilities of their sibling with autism. This can help them understand and appreciate their sibling's differences, and reduce stigma and misunderstanding.

5. Expectations: Set realistic expectations for each child, based on their individual strengths and needs. Avoid comparing siblings to each other or to their peers, and focus on their progress and accomplishments.

6. Inclusion: Encourage inclusion and socialization opportunities for all children, including those with ASD. Provide support and accommodations as needed, and foster a sense of belonging and acceptance.

7. Positive reinforcement: Use positive reinforcement to encourage desired behaviors and skills, and avoid punishment or criticism. This can help build confidence and self-esteem in all children.

In addition to these parenting strategies, siblings of children with ASD may benefit from their own therapies or interventions, such as counseling or social skills training. It is important for parents to recognize and address the unique needs and challenges of each child, and to seek support and guidance when needed.

Managing Stress and Self-Care for Caregivers

Managing Stress and Self-Care for Caregivers of individuals with Autism

Autism Spectrum Disorder (ASD) is a developmental condition that affects social interaction, communication, and behavior. Raising a child with ASD can be challenging and stressful for caregivers. The daily demands of caring for a child with autism can be overwhelming, leading to stress and burnout. Therefore, it is essential to manage stress and engage in self-care activities to maintain optimal physical and mental health. Below we will provide strategies for managing stress and self-care for caregivers of individuals with autism.

Caregivers of individuals with autism experience high levels of stress, which can lead to physical and mental health problems. The stress of caring for a child with autism is often ongoing and can result in chronic stress. Chronic stress can lead to anxiety, depression, fatigue, and sleep disturbances, which can have a significant impact on a caregiver's quality of life. Therefore, it is crucial to find ways to manage stress and engage in self-care activities.

One strategy for managing stress is to practice mindfulness. Mindfulness involves being present and fully engaged in the present moment, without judgment. Mindfulness can be practiced in many ways, including meditation, yoga, or simply taking a walk outside. Mindfulness can reduce stress and anxiety and improve overall well-being.

Another strategy for managing stress is to practice self-compassion. Self-compassion involves treating oneself with kindness, care, and understanding. Caregivers of individuals with autism often put the needs of others before their own, leading to neglect of their own well-being. Practicing self-compassion involves recognizing one's own needs and taking steps to meet those needs.

Engaging in physical activity is an effective strategy for managing stress and improving physical and mental health. Exercise can reduce stress and anxiety, improve sleep quality, and increase energy levels. Caregivers of individuals with autism can incorporate physical activity into their daily routine, such as taking a walk, practicing yoga, or joining a fitness class.

Social support is also essential for managing stress and improving well-being. Caregivers of individuals with autism can benefit from joining support groups or connecting with other caregivers who share similar experiences. Social support can provide emotional and practical assistance, reduce stress, and improve overall well-being.

Self-care activities are also crucial for managing stress and promoting well-being. Self-care involves engaging in activities that promote relaxation, such as taking a warm bath, reading a book, or listening to music. Caregivers of individuals with autism can incorporate self-care activities into their daily routine to promote relaxation and reduce stress.

It is essential to maintain a healthy diet to promote physical and mental well-being. A healthy diet can provide the necessary nutrients to support physical health and energy levels, reducing the risk of physical health problems. A healthy diet can also promote mental health, improving mood and reducing anxiety and depression.

Getting adequate sleep is also crucial for managing stress and promoting well-being. Caregivers of individuals with autism often experience disrupted sleep patterns, leading to fatigue and exhaustion. Getting enough sleep can improve energy levels, mood, and overall well-being.

Chapter Seven

Navigating the Medical System

Navigating the Medical System When Your Child Has Autism

Autism is a complex disorder that can have a significant impact on a child's health and development. As a parent or caregiver, it can be challenging to navigate the medical system when seeking care for a child with autism. From finding the right healthcare providers to communicating effectively with them, here are some tips for navigating the medical system when your child has autism.

Finding the Right Healthcare Providers

One of the first steps in navigating the medical system for your child with autism is finding the right healthcare providers. This may include a primary care physician, specialists such as neurologists or developmental pediatricians, and therapists such as speech and language therapists or occupational therapists.

When looking for healthcare providers, it can be helpful to seek out those who have experience working with children with autism. This may involve asking for recommendations from other parents in the autism community, seeking out support groups or online resources, or contacting local advocacy organizations for recommendations.

It is also important to consider the location and accessibility of healthcare providers. Children with autism may have difficulty with unfamiliar environments or changes to their routine, so finding providers who are close to home or school and have flexible scheduling options may be beneficial.

Communicating with Healthcare Providers

Effective communication with healthcare providers is crucial when seeking care for a child with autism. It is important to share all relevant information about your child's health and development, including any symptoms, behaviors, or concerns you have noticed.

It may be helpful to prepare for appointments by making a list of questions or concerns beforehand, bringing a notebook or recording device to take notes, and bringing any relevant medical records or information.

It is also important to communicate any accommodations or modifications that may be necessary for your child during appointments. For example, you may need to request a quiet room or a shorter appointment time if your child is easily overwhelmed or has difficulty with transitions.

Advocating for Your Child's Needs

Navigating the medical system for a child with autism often requires advocacy on the part of the parent or caregiver. This may involve requesting accommodations or modifications to medical procedures or advocating for appropriate care and services.

Parents and caregivers can advocate for their child's needs by educating themselves about their child's rights and entitlements, staying informed about available services and resources, and communicating their child's needs effectively to healthcare providers.

It may also be helpful to seek out support from advocacy organizations or other parents in the autism community. These groups can provide information, resources, and emotional support to help parents and caregivers navigate the medical system and advocate for their child's needs.

Managing Medical Procedures

Medical procedures can be challenging for children with autism, who may have difficulty with unfamiliar environments, sensory stimuli, or changes to routine. It is important to prepare for medical procedures by communicating with healthcare providers and explaining your child's needs and preferences.

Some strategies that may be helpful for managing medical procedures for children with autism include:

Providing social stories or visual aids to explain what will happen during the procedure

Allowing your child to bring a comfort item or favorite toy to the appointment

Using headphones or earplugs to reduce sensory overload

Providing breaks or opportunities for movement or sensory input as needed

Communicating with healthcare providers about any accommodations or modifications that may be necessary.

Medications and Treatments for Autism

Autism spectrum disorder (ASD) is a complex neurodevelopmental condition that affects communication, social interaction, and behavior. While there is no cure for ASD, there are medications and treatments that can help manage symptoms and improve quality of life for individuals with the disorder. Below we will explore the various medications and treatments available for individuals with ASD.

Medications for Autism:

While there is no single medication that can treat all the symptoms of ASD, some medications can help alleviate certain symptoms. Here are some medications that may be prescribed for individuals with ASD:

1. Antidepressants: Antidepressants are often prescribed for individuals with ASD who have symptoms of anxiety or depression. Selective serotonin reuptake inhibitors (SSRIs) such as fluoxetine (Prozac) and sertraline (Zoloft) are commonly prescribed.

2. Antipsychotics: Antipsychotic medications are sometimes prescribed to help manage symptoms of aggression, self-injury, or severe behavioral problems. Some commonly prescribed antipsychotics for individuals with ASD include risperidone (Risperdal) and aripiprazole (Abilify).

3. Stimulants: Stimulant medications such as methylphenidate (Ritalin) or dextroamphetamine (Dexedrine) may be prescribed for individuals with ASD who have symptoms of hyperactivity or attention-deficit/hyperactivity disorder (ADHD).

4. Anti-anxiety medications: Anti-anxiety medications such as benzodiazepines (Valium, Xanax) may be prescribed for individuals with ASD who have symptoms of anxiety.

It is important to note that while these medications may help alleviate certain symptoms of ASD, they can also have side effects, and their effectiveness varies from person to person. Before starting any medication, it is essential to discuss the risks and benefits with a healthcare provider.

Treatments for Autism:

In addition to medications, there are various treatments available for individuals with ASD. Here are some of the most common treatments:

5. Applied Behavior Analysis (ABA): ABA is a therapy that focuses on teaching new skills and behaviors and reducing undesirable behaviors. ABA involves breaking down complex behaviors into smaller, more manageable steps and using positive reinforcement to encourage the desired behavior.

6. Speech and language therapy: Speech and language therapy can help individuals with ASD develop communication skills. Speech therapy can also help with issues related to voice, fluency, and articulation.

7. Occupational therapy: Occupational therapy can help individuals with ASD develop fine motor skills, sensory processing skills, and activities of daily living such as dressing and grooming.

8. Social skills training: Social skills training involves teaching individuals with ASD social skills such as initiating and maintaining conversations, reading social cues, and making eye contact.

9. Sensory integration therapy: Sensory integration therapy can help individuals with ASD develop sensory processing skills and cope with sensory sensitivities.

10. Educational interventions: Educational interventions such as specialized schooling or tutoring can help individuals with ASD develop academic skills and prepare for the transition to adulthood.

It is important to note that these treatments should be tailored to the individual needs of each person with ASD. What works for one individual may not work for another.

Complementary and Alternative Therapies

Complementary and alternative therapies have gained increasing popularity in recent years as a way to supplement traditional medical treatments for a variety of health conditions, including autism. These therapies, which include a wide range of practices such as herbal remedies, massage, acupuncture, and mindfulness, are often used to help manage symptoms of autism and improve overall well-being.

It's important to note that while complementary and alternative therapies may have some benefits, they are not considered a replacement for evidence-based treatments. Families and individuals with autism should always consult with a healthcare professional before starting any complementary or alternative therapy.

One of the most commonly used complementary therapies for autism is dietary interventions. Many parents of children with autism report that their child's symptoms improve with the elimination of certain foods from their diet, such as gluten and dairy. While there is little scientific evidence to support these claims, some studies have suggested that dietary interventions may be helpful for a subset of individuals with autism. For example, a review of several studies found that a gluten-free and casein-free diet may be effective in improving social and communication skills in some individuals with autism.

Another complementary therapy commonly used for autism is massage therapy. Massage can be a useful tool for individuals with autism who experience sensory difficulties and can be particularly helpful in reducing stress and promoting relaxation. Research has suggested that massage therapy may lead to decreased aggression, hyperactivity, and self-injury in some individuals with autism.

Acupuncture is another complementary therapy that has been used to treat a range of conditions, including autism. While there is limited research on the effectiveness of acupuncture for autism specifically, some studies have suggested that acupuncture may be helpful in reducing some autism-related symptoms, such as hyperactivity and sleep disturbances. However, more research is needed to determine the effectiveness and safety of acupuncture for autism.

Mindfulness and meditation practices are also becoming increasingly popular as complementary therapies for individuals with autism. These practices can help reduce stress and anxiety and promote emotional regulation. A recent study found that a mindfulness-based stress reduction program led to improved social communication skills and decreased anxiety in adolescents with autism.

Other complementary and alternative therapies that have been used for autism include aromatherapy, music therapy, and animal-assisted therapy. While some individuals with autism may find these therapies helpful, there is limited scientific evidence to support their effectiveness.

It's important to note that some complementary and alternative therapies may not be safe or appropriate for individuals with autism. For example, some herbal remedies may interact with prescription medications or have harmful side effects. Additionally, some therapies may not be appropriate for individuals with certain medical conditions or sensory sensitivities.

Co-occurring Conditions and Their Treatment

Co-occurring conditions are quite common in individuals with autism spectrum disorder (ASD). These conditions can have a significant impact on the lives of individuals with ASD and their families. It is important to recognize and understand these conditions, as well as the available treatments and interventions.

Some of the most common co-occurring conditions in individuals with ASD include anxiety disorders, attention deficit hyperactivity disorder (ADHD), depression, and sleep disorders. These conditions can manifest differently in individuals with ASD compared to those without ASD, which can make diagnosis and treatment more challenging.

Anxiety disorders are especially common in individuals with ASD, with up to 40% of individuals with ASD experiencing symptoms of anxiety. Anxiety disorders can present in different ways, such as social anxiety or obsessive-compulsive disorder (OCD). It is important to recognize anxiety in individuals with ASD as it can significantly impact daily life and interfere with the ability to engage in social activities, school or work, and other activities of daily living. Treatment for anxiety disorders in individuals with ASD may include cognitive-behavioral therapy (CBT), medication, or a combination of both.

ADHD is another common co-occurring condition in individuals with ASD, with approximately 30% of individuals with ASD experiencing symptoms of ADHD. ADHD can make it difficult for individuals to focus and pay attention, which can impact academic and social functioning. Treatment for ADHD in individuals with ASD may include medication and/or behavioral interventions.

Depression is also a common co-occurring condition in individuals with ASD, with up to 30% of individuals with ASD experiencing symptoms of depression. Symptoms of depression in individuals with ASD can present differently than in those without ASD, such as increased irritability or aggression. Treatment for depression in individuals with ASD may include medication, CBT, or other psychotherapy.

Sleep disorders are also prevalent in individuals with ASD, with up to 80% of individuals with ASD experiencing sleep difficulties. Sleep disturbances can have a significant impact on daytime functioning and may exacerbate other co-occurring conditions. Treatment for sleep disorders in individuals with ASD may include behavioral interventions, such as sleep hygiene, and medication.

It is important to note that the treatment of co-occurring conditions in individuals with ASD should be individualized and tailored to the specific needs of each individual. Treatment may involve a combination of medication, behavioral interventions, and psychotherapy, and may also involve addressing any sensory sensitivities that may be contributing to the co-occurring condition.

In addition to the aforementioned co-occurring conditions, individuals with ASD may also experience gastrointestinal (GI) issues, seizures, and motor coordination difficulties. These conditions can also impact daily functioning and require appropriate treatment and management.

Chapter Eight

Adult Life with Autism

Autism Spectrum Disorder (ASD) is typically diagnosed in childhood, but individuals with ASD continue to have it throughout their lives. While much of the focus in the ASD community is on early diagnosis and intervention, it is also important to address the needs of individuals with ASD as they transition into adulthood and navigate the challenges of adult life with autism.

One of the major challenges facing adults with autism is finding employment. The unemployment rate for individuals with ASD is high, with some estimates putting it as high as 80%. However, there are organizations and companies that have recognized the unique skills and strengths that individuals with autism can bring to the workplace, such as attention to detail and a strong work ethic. These organizations have developed programs and initiatives to help individuals with autism find and maintain employment.

Another challenge for adults with autism is navigating social relationships. Many individuals with ASD struggle with social interaction and communication, making it difficult to form and maintain friendships and romantic relationships. However, there are support groups and social skills programs designed specifically for individuals with autism, as well as online communities where individuals with autism can connect with others who share their experiences.

In addition to employment and social challenges, there are also healthcare needs that must be addressed for adults with autism. Many individuals with ASD have co-occurring conditions such as anxiety, depression, and gastrointestinal issues, which require specialized treatment and care. It is important for healthcare providers to be knowledgeable about the unique needs and challenges of adults with autism in order to provide effective treatment and support.

Another important aspect of adult life with autism is independence and daily living skills. Many individuals with ASD require support and guidance in areas such as managing finances, cooking, and household chores. There are resources available to help individuals with autism develop these skills and achieve greater independence, such as vocational rehabilitation programs and independent living centers.

Finally, it is important to address the mental and emotional well-being of adults with autism. Many individuals with ASD experience high levels of stress and anxiety, and may benefit from therapies such as cognitive-behavioral therapy or mindfulness practices. Additionally, self-care and stress management techniques such as exercise and relaxation techniques can be helpful in promoting mental and emotional well-being.

Independent Living and Housing Options

Independent living and housing options are important aspects to consider for individuals with autism as they transition to adulthood. While some individuals with autism may have the ability to live independently, others may require more support to live on their own. Additionally, there are a variety of housing options available to individuals with autism that cater to different needs and preferences.

One of the main challenges for individuals with autism who want to live independently is the need for structure and routine. Individuals with autism often thrive in structured environments with predictable routines, and transitioning to an independent living situation can disrupt this stability. To help ease this transition, it may be helpful to gradually increase the level of independence over time, with support from family members, caregivers, or professionals as needed.

For individuals who require more support, group homes or assisted living facilities may be a better option. Group homes are typically residential homes where several individuals with disabilities live together and receive support from staff members. This option can provide individuals with autism with a structured environment and social interaction with peers, while still offering a level of independence. Assisted living facilities are similar to group homes, but may provide additional services and support such as meals, transportation, and housekeeping.

Another housing option for individuals with autism is supportive housing. This type of housing is designed for individuals with disabilities who are able to live independently but require some level of support. Supportive housing can include services such as case management, assistance with household tasks, and help with navigating the community.

For individuals with autism who prefer to live alone, there are also options such as rental apartments or home ownership. However, it is important to consider the level of support needed to ensure that the individual can live independently and manage household tasks such as paying bills, grocery shopping, and maintaining a household.

In addition to housing options, there are also programs and services available to support independent living for individuals with autism. These may include vocational training programs, job coaching services, and life skills training programs. Vocational training programs can provide individuals with the skills and training needed to find and maintain employment. Job coaching services can offer support with job searches, resume writing, and interview preparation. Life skills training programs can provide instruction on important skills such as cooking, cleaning, and managing finances.

One consideration when planning for independent living is the importance of community support. Individuals with autism may have difficulty socializing and forming connections with others, so it is important to identify opportunities for social interaction and community involvement. This may include joining clubs or organizations, volunteering, or participating in community events.

Employment Opportunities and Support

Autism is a neurological disorder that affects an individual's ability to communicate, socialize, and interact with the world around them. While early intervention and therapy are crucial for individuals with autism, adulthood brings with it a new set of challenges, particularly in the realm of employment. Below we will explore the employment opportunities and support available for adults with autism.

According to a report from the Centers for Disease Control and Prevention, only around 1 in 5 individuals with autism are employed. This number is significantly lower than the employment rate for individuals with other disabilities. The reasons for this are complex, but they include challenges related to communication, socialization, and sensory processing.

Fortunately, there are a growing number of employment opportunities and support programs available for adults with autism. One approach that has shown promise is supported employment. Supported employment programs provide ongoing job coaching and support for individuals with disabilities, including autism. This can include help with job searching, training, and accommodations to help individuals perform their job duties.

Another approach is entrepreneurship. Starting a business can be a viable option for individuals with autism who may struggle with traditional employment settings. Entrepreneurs with autism have been successful in a variety of fields, including technology, art, and even agriculture.

In addition to employment opportunities, there are also a variety of support programs available for adults with autism. One such program is vocational rehabilitation, which can provide job training, support, and accommodations to help individuals with autism succeed in the workplace.

Another option is day programs, which provide a structured environment where individuals can participate in vocational training, socialization activities, and other programs to develop skills that will help them in their careers.

It's important to note that many adults with autism may also need support outside of the workplace. This can include assistance with daily living activities such as meal planning, transportation, and personal care.

For individuals with autism who require more intensive support, group homes and residential facilities can provide a safe and supportive environment. These facilities often offer a variety of programs and services designed to help individuals with autism live as independently as possible.

In addition to these programs and services, advocacy organizations and support groups can also be helpful for adults with autism. These groups can provide a sense of community and support, as well as resources and information about available services.

Employment opportunities and support for adults with autism have come a long way in recent years, but there is still much work to be done. Employers and society as a whole must work to better understand and accommodate the needs of individuals with autism. By doing so, we can create a more inclusive and supportive society for all individuals, regardless of their abilities.

Building and Maintaining Relationships

Building and maintaining relationships can be challenging for individuals with autism spectrum disorder (ASD) due to difficulties with social communication and interaction. However, with appropriate support and strategies, it is possible for individuals with ASD to develop meaningful relationships with family, friends, and romantic partners. Below we will explore the challenges of building and maintaining relationships for individuals with ASD, as well as strategies and resources to help them succeed.

One of the main challenges individuals with ASD face when building relationships is the difficulty in understanding and responding appropriately to social cues. They may struggle to interpret body language, facial expressions, and tone of voice, which can lead to misunderstandings or difficulties in communication. Additionally, individuals with ASD may have difficulty initiating and maintaining conversations or understanding the unwritten rules of social interaction, such as taking turns in conversation or interpreting sarcasm and humor.

These challenges can lead to isolation and difficulty forming relationships. However, there are several strategies that can be helpful in building and maintaining relationships for individuals with ASD. One such strategy is social skills training, which can help individuals with ASD learn and practice social communication skills. This training can be provided through therapy sessions, group classes, or individual coaching.

Another strategy is the use of visual supports, such as picture schedules or social stories, to help individuals with ASD understand social situations and expectations. These tools can help individuals with ASD better understand the unwritten rules of social interaction and can provide a framework for them to navigate social situations.

In addition to these strategies, it is also important to provide opportunities for individuals with ASD to socialize with peers and practice their social skills in real-life situations. This can be done through structured social activities such as clubs, sports teams, or other organized groups that provide a safe and supportive environment for individuals with ASD to socialize with others who share similar interests.

It is also important to recognize the importance of relationships with family members and caregivers. Building strong relationships with parents, siblings, and other family members can provide a strong support system for individuals with ASD and can help them develop the skills needed to build relationships with others outside of the family unit.

When it comes to romantic relationships, individuals with ASD may face additional challenges due to difficulties in social communication and understanding the emotional and social cues involved in romantic relationships. However, with appropriate support and strategies, individuals with ASD can develop and maintain meaningful romantic relationships.

One strategy for developing and maintaining romantic relationships for individuals with ASD is the use of online dating websites or apps. These platforms can provide a less overwhelming way to meet potential partners and can allow individuals with ASD to take their time getting to know someone before meeting in person.

It is also important to provide education and support to both individuals with ASD and their partners. Educating partners about the unique challenges and strengths of individuals with ASD can help them better understand and communicate with their partner. Additionally, providing individual and couples therapy can be helpful in addressing any relationship challenges and developing strategies for successful communication and conflict resolution.

Chapter Nine

Advocacy and Support

Autism Spectrum Disorder (ASD) is a complex developmental disorder that affects communication, social interaction, and behavior. The condition is characterized by a range of symptoms that can vary widely in severity and presentation from person to person. Those with autism may have difficulty with social cues, communication, and repetitive behaviors. Because of these difficulties, they may need extra support from family, friends, and professionals to navigate their way through life. This is where advocacy and support come into play.

Advocacy is the process of speaking up and taking action on behalf of oneself or others. For those with autism, advocacy can be a crucial tool for ensuring that they receive the support and services they need. It can involve everything from seeking out resources and information to fighting for better policies and programs.

One of the most important types of advocacy for individuals with autism is self-advocacy. This means learning how to advocate for oneself and one's needs. It involves understanding one's own strengths and challenges, identifying what support is needed, and communicating those needs effectively. It can be a challenging process, but it is essential for individuals with autism to learn how to advocate for themselves as they move into adulthood.

Another important aspect of advocacy is supporting others. Parents, siblings, and caregivers of those with autism can be strong advocates for their loved ones. They can help ensure that their loved one's needs are met and that they receive the appropriate services and support. This can involve everything from advocating for an appropriate educational program to fighting for better insurance coverage.

Support can come in many forms. One of the most important types of support is emotional support. Individuals with autism may face social isolation and other challenges, which can lead to feelings of loneliness and anxiety. It is important for family members and friends to provide emotional support and help their loved one build connections with others.

Another important type of support is practical support. This can include everything from helping with daily activities such as cooking and cleaning to providing transportation to appointments and activities. Practical support can also involve advocating for services and support that can help the individual with autism thrive.

In addition to family and friends, there are many organizations and professionals who provide advocacy and support for individuals with autism. These can include autism advocacy organizations, support groups, and professionals such as special education teachers, occupational therapists, and speech therapists. These individuals and organizations can provide valuable resources, information, and guidance on everything from legal rights to accessing services and support.

One of the most important things to remember about advocacy and support is that it is an ongoing process. As individuals with autism grow and change, their needs may change as well. Advocates and supporters must be willing to adapt and adjust their approach to meet the individual's evolving needs.

Resources for Families and Individuals with Autism

Autism spectrum disorder (ASD) is a complex neurodevelopmental disorder that affects communication, social interaction, and behavior. It can be challenging for families and individuals with autism to navigate the resources and support available to them. However, there are many resources available that can help families and individuals with autism to manage their condition and live their best lives. Below we will explore some of the resources that are available to families and individuals with autism.

One of the most important resources for families and individuals with autism is education. There are many educational resources available, including special education programs in schools, online courses, and training programs for parents and caregivers. These resources can help individuals with autism to develop skills and strategies for managing their condition, as well as provide support and guidance for parents and caregivers.

Another important resource for families and individuals with autism is therapy. There are many types of therapy available for individuals with autism, including behavioral therapy, speech and language therapy, and occupational therapy. These therapies can help individuals with autism to improve their communication and social skills, manage their behavior, and develop new skills.

In addition to therapy, there are also many support groups and organizations that provide resources and support for families and individuals with autism. These groups can provide a sense of community and connection for families and individuals with autism, as well as offer information about available resources and support services.

Technology can also be a valuable resource for families and individuals with autism. There are many apps and software programs available that can help individuals with autism to improve their communication and social skills, manage their behavior, and develop new skills. These technologies can also provide support and guidance for parents and caregivers, and can help to reduce stress and improve quality of life for families and individuals with autism.

One of the most important resources for families and individuals with autism is advocacy. There are many organizations and advocacy groups that work to raise awareness about autism, promote research, and advocate for policies and legislation that support individuals with autism and their families. These organizations can also provide support and guidance for families and individuals with autism who are navigating the legal and educational systems.

Finally, it is important to recognize the role that families and individuals with autism play in advocating for themselves and others. By sharing their experiences and stories, families and individuals with autism can raise awareness about the challenges they face and help to break down stereotypes and stigmas associated with autism.

Building a Support Network

Building a Support Network

Autism is a complex neurodevelopmental disorder that affects individuals in a variety of ways. The challenges of autism can be significant, and individuals with autism and their families often require a great deal of support. Building a strong support network is essential for individuals with autism to thrive and reach their full potential. Below we will discuss the importance of building a support network, as well as strategies for creating one.

Why is Building a Support Network Important?

Building a support network is important for several reasons. First, individuals with autism may require a variety of services and support throughout their lives. These may include medical care, therapy, and educational support. By building a support network, individuals with autism and their families can access these services more easily and efficiently.

In addition, a support network can provide emotional support and social connections. Autism can be isolating for individuals and families, and a support network can provide a sense of community and belonging. Social support can also help individuals with autism to build their social skills and improve their relationships with others.

Finally, a support network can provide advocacy and empowerment. Advocacy is critical for individuals with autism, as they may face discrimination and barriers to accessing services and opportunities. A support network can provide advocacy and empower individuals with autism to speak up for themselves and their rights.

Strategies for Building a Support Network

There are several strategies for building a support network for individuals with autism and their families. These include:

1. Joining support groups: There are many support groups available for individuals with autism and their families. These groups provide an opportunity to connect with others who are going through similar experiences, share information and resources, and provide emotional support. There are support groups online, as well as in-person groups that meet regularly.

2. Finding a mentor: A mentor can be an invaluable resource for individuals with autism and their families. A mentor is someone who has experience navigating the challenges of autism and can provide guidance and support.

Mentors can be found through support groups, advocacy organizations, or through personal networks.

3. Seeking out professional support: Individuals with autism may require a variety of professional support services, such as medical care, therapy, and educational support. Building relationships with professionals who specialize in autism can provide a valuable resource for individuals and families.

4. Getting involved in advocacy: Advocacy is critical for individuals with autism and their families. Getting involved in advocacy organizations and activities can provide opportunities to advocate for services and supports, as well as connect with others who are working towards similar goals.

5. Building personal networks: Building personal networks can provide a sense of community and social support. This can include friends, family members, and neighbors who can provide practical support, such as transportation or assistance with daily tasks.

Challenges and Solutions

Building a support network can be challenging, particularly for individuals and families who live in areas with limited resources or who face social isolation. However, there are solutions to these challenges.

For example, online support groups can provide an opportunity to connect with others who live in different geographic areas. Additionally, advocacy organizations may provide resources and connections to services and support that are not available locally.

In some cases, it may be necessary to be creative and build support networks outside of traditional channels. For example, individuals with autism may benefit from connecting with others who share their interests or hobbies, such as through clubs or groups related to music, art, or other activities.

Advocating for Autism Awareness and Acceptance

Autism spectrum disorder (ASD) is a neurodevelopmental disorder that affects communication, social interaction, and behavior. It is estimated that 1 in 54 children in the United States is diagnosed with ASD, making it one of the most common neurodevelopmental disorders. Despite its prevalence, many people still have limited understanding of what autism is and how it affects individuals.

Advocacy for autism awareness and acceptance is crucial for creating a more inclusive and understanding society for individuals with autism. Below we will discuss the importance of advocating for autism awareness and acceptance, the benefits of increased awareness and acceptance, and how individuals can advocate for autism awareness and acceptance.

Advocating for autism awareness and acceptance is important for several reasons. Firstly, it helps to reduce stigma and discrimination towards individuals with autism. Many people with autism face social isolation, bullying, and discrimination due to their differences. Raising awareness about autism can help to combat these negative attitudes and behaviors by promoting understanding and acceptance.

Secondly, advocating for autism awareness and acceptance can lead to increased access to resources and support for individuals with autism and their families. This can include access to educational programs, therapies, and community services that can help individuals with autism to thrive.

Lastly, promoting autism awareness and acceptance can help to increase research funding for autism. Research on autism is crucial for understanding the causes of autism and developing effective treatments and interventions.

Increased awareness and acceptance of autism can have numerous benefits for individuals with autism and their families. When people understand the unique strengths and challenges of individuals with autism, they are more likely to appreciate their differences and value their contributions. This can lead to increased inclusion in social settings, education, and employment.

Furthermore, when individuals with autism are accepted and supported, they are more likely to reach their full potential. With access to appropriate resources and support, individuals with autism can learn and grow in their own unique way, achieving success and happiness in their own way.

So, how can individuals advocate for autism awareness and acceptance? There are several ways to get involved:

1. Share information about autism: Share articles, videos, and personal stories about autism on social media to raise awareness and increase understanding.

2. Participate in autism-related events: Attend events that promote autism awareness and acceptance, such as autism walks, fundraisers, and conferences.

3. Educate others: Educate family members, friends, and colleagues about autism and how they can support individuals with autism.

4. Support autism organizations: Donate to autism organizations that provide support, resources, and advocacy for individuals with autism and their families.

5. Be an ally: Show support for individuals with autism by being an ally and advocating for their rights and inclusion.

Chapter Ten

Autism in the Media and Society

Autism is a developmental disorder that affects communication, social interaction, and behavior. It is a lifelong condition, but early intervention and support can help individuals with autism lead fulfilling lives. Despite increased awareness and understanding of autism in recent years, many misconceptions still exist, and people with autism continue to face stigma and discrimination. Below we will explore the portrayal of autism in the media and society and its impact on individuals with autism and their families.

In the media, people with autism are often depicted as savants or geniuses with exceptional skills, such as in the popular movie "Rain Man." While it is true that some individuals with autism possess unique talents and abilities, this portrayal can be misleading and does not represent the full spectrum of autism. In reality, individuals with autism may have a wide range of abilities and challenges, and each person's experience is unique.

Media portrayals of autism also tend to focus on the challenges and difficulties associated with the condition. News stories often depict individuals with autism as violent or aggressive, which is a harmful stereotype that does not accurately represent most people with autism. This negative portrayal can contribute to fear and misunderstanding of autism and lead to discrimination and prejudice.

Society's understanding of autism has come a long way in recent years, but stigma and discrimination still exist. Many people with autism and their families face isolation and exclusion from their communities, and there is a lack of understanding and support for their unique needs. Education and awareness are key to changing this and creating a more inclusive society.

One way to promote autism awareness and acceptance is to encourage more positive representation of autism in the media. This includes sharing stories of individuals with autism who are living fulfilling lives and making valuable contributions to society. By highlighting their achievements and strengths, we can help break down stereotypes and increase understanding of autism.

Another important aspect of promoting acceptance is to provide support and resources to individuals with autism and their families. This includes access to early intervention and specialized services to help them reach their full potential. It also includes creating inclusive environments that value and respect the unique abilities and perspectives of people with autism.

Advocacy is also critical in promoting autism awareness and acceptance. This involves speaking out against harmful stereotypes and discrimination and advocating for policies and programs that support individuals with autism and their families. Advocates can work with policymakers, educators, and community leaders to create more inclusive environments and increase access to services and resources.

Portrayals of Autism in Film and Television

Portrayals of Autism in Film and Television

Autism is a neurological disorder that affects communication and social interaction. Over the years, autism has been portrayed in film and television in various ways, ranging from highly accurate depictions to inaccurate and stereotypical portrayals. The portrayal of autism in media can have a significant impact on how society perceives and understands the disorder. Below we will explore the history of autism in film and television, examine the accuracy and impact of these portrayals, and discuss the importance of accurate representation.

The first notable portrayal of autism in film was in the 1988 movie "Rain Man," which won four Oscars, including Best Picture. The film starred Tom Cruise as a man named Charlie Babbitt, who learns that he has an older brother named Raymond (Dustin Hoffman) who has autism. The film is widely credited with increasing public awareness of autism and was seen as a groundbreaking portrayal of the disorder.

"Rain Man" was followed by a series of other films that featured characters with autism. These include "Mozart and the Whale," "The Story of Luke," and "Temple Grandin." These films were praised for their realistic and compassionate portrayal of autism, with actors such as Claire Danes in "Temple Grandin" receiving critical acclaim for their performances.

While some films have accurately depicted autism, others have been criticized for their portrayal of the disorder. One such film is "The Accountant," which starred Ben Affleck as an accountant with autism who also happens to be a highly skilled assassin. Critics have argued that the film perpetuates the stereotype of individuals with autism being savants, a notion that is not representative of the vast majority of individuals on the autism spectrum.

Television has also played a role in portraying autism. Shows such as "Atypical," "The Good Doctor," and "Parenthood" have all featured characters with autism, with varying degrees of accuracy. "Atypical" has been criticized for its stereotypical portrayal of autism, with many in the autism community arguing that the show relies too heavily on outdated and inaccurate stereotypes.

"The Good Doctor," on the other hand, has been praised for its portrayal of an individual with autism who is also a talented surgeon. The show has been praised for accurately portraying the challenges that individuals with autism face in the workplace and for showing that individuals with autism can excel in their chosen fields.

The impact of these portrayals can be significant. Films and television shows can shape public perception and understanding of autism. Accurate portrayals can increase understanding and acceptance of the disorder, while inaccurate portrayals can perpetuate stereotypes and myths about autism. It is essential that individuals with autism are portrayed in a fair, accurate, and compassionate manner.

Moreover, media portrayals of autism can have an impact on the individuals with autism themselves. Many individuals with autism report feeling isolated and misunderstood. Seeing accurate portrayals of autism on screen can provide them with a sense of validation and representation. It can also encourage them to embrace their identity and feel more comfortable in their own skin.

The Role of Social Media in Autism Advocacy

The use of social media in autism advocacy has been rapidly increasing in recent years. Social media provides a platform for individuals with autism and their families to connect with each other, share their stories and experiences, and raise awareness about autism spectrum disorder (ASD). Below we will explore the role of social media in autism advocacy, including its benefits and challenges.

One of the primary benefits of social media in autism advocacy is the ability to connect with others who have similar experiences. Parents of children with autism often feel isolated and alone, but through social media, they can connect with other parents who are going through the same challenges. This can provide a sense of community and support, which can be invaluable in navigating the often complex world of autism.

Social media can also be a powerful tool for raising awareness about ASD. By sharing their stories and experiences on social media, individuals with autism and their families can educate others about the disorder and promote acceptance and understanding. Social media campaigns such as Autism Speaks' "Light It Up Blue" and the National Autism Association's "Autism Awareness Month" have helped to raise awareness about autism on a global scale.

Another benefit of social media in autism advocacy is the ability to advocate for policy changes. Social media campaigns can help to raise awareness about issues such as the lack of funding for autism research or the need for better support services for individuals with autism. Advocacy efforts on social media have been successful in bringing about policy changes at the local, state, and federal levels.

Despite these benefits, there are also challenges associated with the use of social media in autism advocacy. One of the biggest challenges is the potential for misinformation and the spread of false information about autism. Social media can be a breeding ground for conspiracy theories and pseudoscientific claims about autism, which can be harmful and misleading.

Another challenge is the potential for cyberbullying and online harassment. Individuals with autism are particularly vulnerable to online bullying due to difficulties with social communication and interaction. Cyberbullying can cause significant emotional distress and can have long-lasting effects on mental health.

Furthermore, social media can be overwhelming and exhausting for individuals with autism and their families. The constant barrage of information, opinions, and updates can be difficult to process, leading to sensory overload and increased stress levels. It is important for individuals with autism and their families to take breaks from social media when needed and to prioritize self-care.

Misconceptions and Stereotypes Surrounding Autism

Autism Spectrum Disorder (ASD) is a developmental disorder that affects communication, social interaction, and behavior. Despite being a relatively common condition, ASD is still surrounded by misconceptions and stereotypes that can cause harm to individuals on the spectrum and their families. Below we will explore some of the most prevalent misconceptions and stereotypes surrounding autism and their impact.

One of the most common misconceptions surrounding autism is that it is a rare condition. In reality, ASD is estimated to affect 1 in 54 children in the United States alone. However, this misconception persists because of the lack of visibility of individuals on the spectrum in mainstream media and society. This lack of representation leads to a general lack of understanding about what autism is and what it means to be on the spectrum.

Another misconception surrounding autism is that it is a disorder that only affects children. While the symptoms of autism are typically first noticed in childhood, ASD is a lifelong condition. Individuals on the spectrum continue to experience challenges with social interaction, communication, and behavior throughout their lives. This misconception can lead to a lack of support for adults on the spectrum and a lack of understanding about the challenges they face.

There is also a common stereotype that individuals on the autism spectrum lack empathy or are incapable of forming meaningful relationships. This stereotype is not only untrue but harmful. Many individuals on the spectrum have deep and meaningful relationships with others, and while they may struggle with social interaction, this does not mean that they are incapable of empathy. This stereotype can lead to misunderstandings about the emotional experiences of individuals on the spectrum, which can further exacerbate feelings of isolation and loneliness.

Another stereotype surrounding autism is that individuals on the spectrum are all geniuses or savants. While some individuals with autism have exceptional skills in certain areas, such as math or music, this is not true for everyone on the spectrum. This stereotype can be harmful because it can create unrealistic expectations for individuals on the spectrum and lead to feelings of inadequacy when they do not live up to these expectations.

One of the most damaging stereotypes surrounding autism is that it is caused by bad parenting or a lack of discipline. This belief is not only untrue but can cause immense harm to families and individuals on the spectrum. The cause of autism is still not fully understood, but it is believed to be a combination of genetic and environmental factors. Blaming parents or individuals with autism for their condition can lead to feelings of guilt, shame, and self-blame, which can have long-lasting effects on mental health.

These misconceptions and stereotypes surrounding autism can have a significant impact on individuals on the spectrum and their families. They can lead to a lack of understanding and support from society, which can further exacerbate feelings of isolation and exclusion. It is important for individuals to educate themselves about autism and challenge these misconceptions and stereotypes to create a more inclusive and accepting society for all.

Chapter Eleven

Autism and Technology

Autism spectrum disorder (ASD) is a complex developmental disorder that affects a person's ability to communicate, socialize and engage in repetitive behaviors. The diagnosis of autism has increased dramatically in recent years, with current estimates suggesting that 1 in 54 children in the United States have ASD. Although there is no known cure for autism, there are many treatments and therapies that can help individuals with ASD to improve their quality of life. One area where technology has made a significant impact is in the treatment and management of autism.

One of the ways in which technology has benefited individuals with autism is through the use of assistive technologies. These technologies are designed to help people with disabilities to perform tasks that may be challenging for them. For example, communication apps such as Proloquo2Go and TouchChat allow nonverbal individuals to communicate using pictures and symbols. This can significantly improve their ability to communicate with others and make their needs known. Similarly, other assistive technologies such as visual aids and sensory devices can help individuals with autism to better understand their environment and engage in more meaningful social interactions.

Another way in which technology has helped individuals with autism is through the use of virtual reality (VR) and augmented reality (AR) technologies. These technologies can be used to create simulated environments that allow individuals with autism to practice and develop social and communication skills in a safe and controlled environment. For example, VR systems can be used to create simulations of social situations, such as job interviews or public speaking, that can help individuals with autism to develop the skills they need to succeed in these situations. Similarly, AR technologies can be used to create visual aids that can help individuals with autism to better understand their surroundings and navigate their environment.

In addition to assistive technologies and VR/AR technologies, there are also many apps and software programs that have been developed specifically for individuals with autism. These programs can help individuals with autism to develop a variety of skills, including communication, social interaction, and executive functioning. For example, the app "Autism Tracker" allows parents and caregivers to track and monitor their child's progress in various areas, including communication, social skills, and behavior. Similarly, the software program "Brain Power" uses AI technology to help individuals with autism to develop social and emotional skills through interactive games and activities.

One of the challenges in the use of technology for autism is ensuring that the technology is accessible to everyone. Many individuals with autism may have limited access to technology or may not have the resources to purchase expensive devices or software programs. To address this issue, there are many organizations that provide free or low-cost assistive technologies and software programs to individuals with autism and their families. For example, the Autism Speaks website provides a list of free assistive technologies and apps that can be used by individuals with autism.

Despite the many benefits of technology in the treatment and management of autism, there are also concerns about the potential negative effects of technology use. Some studies have suggested that excessive screen time can have negative effects on social skills and language development in young children. Additionally, there is concern that the use of technology may lead to social isolation and a lack of face-to-face interactions.

Assistive Technology for Communication and Learning

Assistive technology has become an integral part of the lives of individuals with autism spectrum disorder (ASD) as it can help to address communication and learning challenges. This technology can be defined as any device, software, or equipment that helps individuals with disabilities to perform tasks that they would not be able to perform otherwise. Below we will explore the various types of assistive technology that are available for individuals with ASD, how they work, and the benefits they provide.

One of the most commonly used types of assistive technology for communication is augmentative and alternative communication (AAC) devices. These devices are designed to support communication for individuals who are nonverbal or have difficulty communicating verbally. AAC devices can range from simple picture communication boards to high-tech speech-generating devices. Picture communication boards are typically made up of a series of images or symbols that represent words or phrases, and the user can point to the pictures to communicate their message. In contrast, speech-generating devices use a touch screen or buttons to produce spoken language.

Another type of assistive technology for communication is social skills training software. This software can help individuals with ASD learn and practice social skills, which is often a challenge for individuals with ASD. The software can include interactive games, video models, and other multimedia resources that provide visual and auditory feedback to help individuals develop social skills.

For individuals with ASD who struggle with reading, writing, or other academic skills, there are several types of assistive technology available. For example, text-to-speech software can read written material out loud to the user, making it easier for them to comprehend and retain the information. Similarly, speech-to-text software can convert spoken language into written text, making it easier for individuals who struggle with writing to communicate their thoughts.

There are also a variety of sensory and motor assistive technologies available for individuals with ASD. Sensory integration therapy is one approach that can help individuals with sensory processing challenges. This therapy may involve the use of weighted blankets or vests, sensory bins filled with different textures, or sensory swings. These tools can help to provide sensory input that helps to regulate an individual's sensory system. Similarly, motor assistive technology, such as adaptive writing tools or assistive devices for grooming, can help individuals with fine motor challenges to perform daily tasks.

Assistive technology can have a significant impact on the lives of individuals with ASD. By addressing communication, social, academic, sensory, and motor challenges, assistive technology can help individuals with ASD to increase their independence and improve their quality of life. Additionally, assistive technology can help to reduce frustration and anxiety, which can be common for individuals with ASD who struggle with these challenges.

The Role of Teletherapy in Autism Support

The world of healthcare has seen a lot of advancements in recent years, and one of the most notable has been the rise of teletherapy. Teletherapy involves receiving therapy sessions through video conferencing rather than in-person visits. It has many benefits, including convenience, accessibility, and cost-effectiveness. For individuals on the autism spectrum, teletherapy can be an especially useful tool for receiving support and treatment.

Autism spectrum disorder (ASD) is a neurodevelopmental disorder that affects communication, social interaction, and behavior. Children and adults with ASD often require therapy to help them navigate the challenges of everyday life. However, many families face barriers to accessing traditional in-person therapy, such as distance, cost, or lack of qualified providers in their area. This is where teletherapy can play a crucial role in helping individuals with autism receive the support they need.

One of the biggest advantages of teletherapy for individuals with autism is that it can be conducted from the comfort of their own home. This is especially important for children on the autism spectrum, who may struggle with transitions and new environments. Teletherapy can provide a sense of stability and consistency, which can be comforting to children with ASD.

Another benefit of teletherapy is that it can be tailored to the unique needs of each individual. For example, some individuals with ASD may struggle with sensory issues, making traditional in-person therapy difficult. Teletherapy can be adjusted to meet the specific sensory needs of each person, such as adjusting lighting or sound levels. This level of customization can be difficult to achieve in a traditional therapy setting.

Teletherapy can also help to increase access to qualified providers for individuals with autism. Many families in rural or remote areas may not have access to specialized providers, making it difficult to receive appropriate treatment. Teletherapy can connect families with providers from anywhere in the world, making it easier to access the support they need.

There are several types of teletherapy that may be beneficial for individuals with autism. One example is telebehavioral therapy, which involves video conferencing with a behavioral therapist. This type of therapy can be used to address challenging behaviors or to help individuals develop social skills. Another example is teleoccupational therapy, which can help individuals with ASD improve fine motor skills and develop activities of daily living (ADL) skills.

It is important to note that teletherapy is not appropriate for everyone. Individuals with more severe autism symptoms may require in-person therapy or a combination of teletherapy and in-person therapy. Additionally, not all insurance plans cover teletherapy, so families may need to pay out of pocket for these services.

Despite these limitations, teletherapy has the potential to revolutionize the way that individuals with autism receive support and treatment. As technology continues to advance, teletherapy may become an increasingly important tool in helping individuals with autism reach their full potential.

Mobile Applications and Tools for Autism

Mobile applications and tools have revolutionized many aspects of our lives, and the world of autism support is no exception. There is a growing number of mobile apps available that offer a range of resources and tools for individuals with autism, their families, and professionals who work with them. These apps can help with everything from communication and social skills to learning and behavior management.

One of the most significant advantages of mobile apps for autism support is their accessibility. Many of these apps are available for free or at a low cost, making them much more accessible to families who may not have access to other resources or therapy services. Additionally, mobile apps can be used anytime and anywhere, providing more flexibility and convenience for families who may have busy schedules or limited access to therapy services.

There are many different types of mobile apps available for autism support, each with its own unique features and benefits. Here are some of the most popular categories:

1. Communication Apps: One of the most significant challenges for individuals with autism is communication. Communication apps can help individuals with autism express themselves and communicate their wants and needs more effectively. Some of these apps use pictures or symbols to help individuals communicate, while others use voice output or text-to-speech technology.

2. Social Skills Apps: Many individuals with autism struggle with social skills and may have difficulty making friends or understanding social cues. Social skills apps can help individuals with autism practice social skills in a safe and controlled environment. These apps may include games or simulations that teach social skills or provide opportunities to practice social interactions.

3. Learning Apps: Learning apps can help individuals with autism develop academic skills and improve their overall learning. These apps may include educational games or interactive tools that make learning more engaging and accessible for individuals with autism.

4. Behavioral Management Apps: Behavioral management apps can help parents and caregivers manage challenging behaviors in individuals with autism. These apps may include tools for tracking behaviors or providing strategies for managing behavior in real-time.

While mobile apps for autism support can be helpful, it's essential to note that they should not replace therapy services or other forms of professional support. These apps can be used in conjunction with therapy services or as a supplement to other forms of support.

It's also important to note that not all mobile apps for autism support are created equal. Some apps may not be evidence-based or may not have been tested for efficacy. Families should do their research and consult with professionals to ensure they are using high-quality apps that are appropriate for their child's needs.

Here are some examples of popular mobile apps for autism support:

5. Proloquo2Go: Proloquo2Go is a communication app that uses symbols and pictures to help individuals with autism communicate. The app also includes a text-to-speech feature that allows individuals to express themselves using their own words.

6. Autism Track: Autism Track is a behavioral management app that allows parents and caregivers to track behaviors and identify patterns in behavior over time. The app also provides resources and strategies for managing challenging behaviors.

7. Autism iHelp: Autism iHelp is a learning app that includes a variety of educational games and activities designed to help individuals with autism develop academic and language skills.

8. Model Me Going Places: Model Me Going Places is a social skills app that includes videos and simulations designed to teach social skills in real-life settings, such as going to the grocery store or the doctor's office.

Mobile apps and tools have the potential to make a significant difference in the lives of individuals with autism and their families. By providing accessible and affordable resources for communication, social skills, learning, and behavioral management, these apps can help individuals with autism reach their full potential and live more fulfilling lives. However, it's important to use these apps in conjunction with therapy services and consult with professionals to ensure they are appropriate and effective for each individual's unique needs.

The Importance of Early Intervention

The earlier autism is diagnosed, the earlier interventions can begin, which can have a significant impact on the child's development and future success. Early intervention is the key to ensuring that children with autism can reach their full potential and lead a fulfilling life.

Early intervention is an approach that involves identifying children who may be at risk of autism spectrum disorder (ASD) as early as possible, and then providing targeted interventions to support their development. Early intervention programs are designed to provide children with the skills they need to interact with others, communicate effectively, and manage their behaviors.

The importance of early intervention cannot be overstated. Children who receive early intervention services are more likely to develop better communication and social skills, which are essential for success in school and in later life. Early intervention can help reduce challenging behaviors, which can reduce the risk of developing other problems, such as anxiety, depression, and attention deficit hyperactivity disorder (ADHD).

There are many different types of interventions that may be used in early intervention programs, depending on the child's specific needs. For example, speech therapy may be used to help children with communication difficulties, while behavioral therapy may be used to help children with challenging behaviors. Occupational therapy may be used to help children with sensory processing difficulties or motor skills issues.

One of the primary benefits of early intervention is that it provides parents and caregivers with the tools they need to support their child's development. Parents can learn techniques for managing challenging behaviors, providing structure and routine, and supporting their child's social and emotional development. They can also learn how to work with educators and healthcare professionals to ensure that their child's needs are met.

Early intervention programs are typically delivered in a variety of settings, including home-based programs, daycare centers, and schools. These programs may involve one-on-one therapy sessions, group therapy sessions, or a combination of both. Some programs may also include parent training, which can help parents better understand their child's needs and how to support their development.

It is important to note that early intervention is not a cure for autism. Rather, it is a way to provide children with the support they need to develop the skills they need to succeed. With the right interventions and support, children with autism can lead fulfilling lives and achieve their goals.

Chapter Twelve

Identifying Autism in Infants and Toddlers

Identifying Autism in Infants and Toddlers

Autism spectrum disorder (ASD) is a neurodevelopmental disorder that affects communication, social interaction, and behavior. Early identification of ASD is crucial for providing interventions and support to improve outcomes for individuals with the disorder. While ASD is typically diagnosed between the ages of two and four, early signs and symptoms can be observed in infants and toddlers. Below we will explore the importance of identifying autism in infants and toddlers, the early signs and symptoms of ASD, and the diagnostic process for young children.

The importance of early identification of autism cannot be overstated. Research has shown that early intervention can significantly improve outcomes for children with ASD. Early interventions, such as applied behavior analysis (ABA), speech therapy, and occupational therapy, can improve communication skills, social skills, and behavior. Additionally, early identification allows families to access resources and support systems that can help them navigate the challenges of raising a child with ASD. Early identification and intervention also allow families to begin to adjust to their child's diagnosis and develop coping strategies.

Identifying ASD in infants and toddlers can be challenging, as some signs and symptoms may be subtle or appear to be typical developmental milestones. However, there are some early signs and symptoms that parents and caregivers can look for. These signs may include a lack of response to their name, a lack of eye contact, a lack of interest in social interaction or play, delayed language development or loss of language skills, repetitive behaviors, and sensory sensitivities.

Infants and toddlers with ASD may also exhibit delayed gross motor and fine motor skills, such as crawling, walking, and using utensils. They may have difficulty with transitions or changes in routine, and may become fixated on certain objects or activities. Some infants and toddlers with ASD may also have difficulty regulating their emotions, and may experience frequent tantrums or meltdowns.

If parents or caregivers suspect that their infant or toddler may have ASD, it is important to seek an evaluation from a qualified healthcare professional. The diagnostic process for young children typically involves a comprehensive assessment that includes observation and evaluation of developmental milestones, communication skills, social interaction, and behavior. The assessment may also include hearing and vision tests, as well as genetic testing to rule out other conditions that may cause similar symptoms.

There are several screening tools and diagnostic tests that healthcare professionals may use to evaluate infants and toddlers for ASD. The Modified Checklist for Autism in Toddlers (M-CHAT) is a widely used screening tool that can be completed by parents or caregivers to help identify early signs of ASD. The Autism Diagnostic Observation Schedule (ADOS) is a diagnostic test that is used to evaluate social communication skills and behavior in individuals with ASD. Other diagnostic tests may include cognitive and developmental assessments, as well as medical evaluations to rule out other conditions.

In addition to seeking a formal evaluation, parents and caregivers can also work with their child's healthcare professional to monitor developmental milestones and seek support and resources. Early intervention services, such as speech therapy and occupational therapy, can begin as soon as an ASD diagnosis is suspected, and can be provided in a variety of settings, including in the home, at school, and in clinical settings. Families can also seek support from local and national organizations that provide information, resources, and advocacy for individuals with ASD and their families.

Early Intervention Programs and Their Benefits

Early intervention programs are critical in providing young children with Autism Spectrum Disorder (ASD) the support they need to reach their full potential. These programs, which typically begin before the age of three, involve a range of interventions aimed at improving a child's social, communication, and cognitive abilities. Below we will explore the benefits of early intervention programs for children with ASD.

The earlier a child with ASD receives intervention, the more likely they are to benefit from it. Research has shown that intensive interventions that start before the age of three can significantly improve a child's cognitive and language abilities. These early interventions can also help children with ASD develop social skills and improve their ability to communicate with others. Furthermore, early intervention programs can reduce the need for special education services later in life and can even lead to the child being able to live independently as an adult.

Early intervention programs are tailored to the individual needs of each child with ASD. The intervention team will work with the child and their family to identify areas where the child needs support and develop a plan to address those needs. These plans often involve a combination of therapies, including applied behavior analysis (ABA), speech and language therapy, and occupational therapy.

ABA is one of the most widely used therapies in early intervention programs. This therapy is based on the principles of behaviorism and involves breaking down complex skills into smaller, more manageable parts. The child is then taught these skills through a series of positive reinforcements. ABA is particularly effective in improving language and social skills in children with ASD.

Speech and language therapy is another critical component of early intervention programs. This therapy is designed to help children with ASD improve their communication skills, including speech, language, and social communication. Speech and language therapy can help children with ASD learn how to initiate and maintain conversations, as well as understand the social rules of communication.

Occupational therapy can also be beneficial in early intervention programs. This therapy is designed to help children with ASD develop the fine motor skills they need to complete everyday tasks, such as dressing and feeding themselves. Occupational therapy can also help children with ASD learn how to regulate their sensory input and develop coping mechanisms for sensory overload.

Early intervention programs also involve parent training and support. Parents are a critical part of the intervention team, and they play a vital role in helping their child develop the skills they need to succeed. Parent training can include teaching parents how to use positive reinforcement to encourage their child's development, as well as how to recognize and respond to their child's needs.

Strategies for Supporting Early Development

Strategies for Supporting Early Development

Early childhood is a critical period of development for children, and it is especially important for children with autism spectrum disorder (ASD). During this time, children with ASD require early and intensive intervention to promote social communication, language, and cognitive development. While every child with ASD is unique and has different strengths and challenges, there are some strategies that parents, caregivers, and educators can use to support early development and promote positive outcomes.

One of the most important strategies for supporting early development in children with ASD is to provide a structured and predictable environment. Children with ASD often have difficulty understanding and adapting to changes in routine, so maintaining a consistent schedule can help them feel more comfortable and secure. This can include consistent meal times, nap times, and play times, as well as a consistent daily routine. Visual schedules and social stories can also be helpful for children with ASD, as they provide a clear and predictable sequence of events.

Another strategy for supporting early development in children with ASD is to use a strengths-based approach. Children with ASD often have unique talents and interests, and these should be encouraged and nurtured. For example, a child who has a strong interest in trains could be provided with books, toys, and activities that relate to trains, which can help them develop vocabulary, improve their social communication skills, and promote imaginative play.

Communication is a key area of development for children with ASD, and there are many strategies that can be used to promote language development. One effective strategy is to use a communication system that is tailored to the child's strengths and preferences. This might include visual supports, such as picture cards or a communication app on a tablet, or a sign language system. Providing plenty of opportunities for social interaction and play can also help to promote language development.

Play is an important part of childhood, and it is especially important for children with ASD. However, children with ASD may have difficulty engaging in imaginative or cooperative play, so it is important to provide opportunities for structured play. For example, providing toys or activities that involve turn-taking or joint attention can help children with ASD learn social communication skills and develop a sense of shared play.

Social skills are another key area of development for children with ASD, and there are many strategies that can be used to promote social interaction. One effective strategy is to use social stories or role-playing to teach social skills in a structured and supportive environment. Another effective strategy is to provide opportunities for social interaction with peers, such as play dates or structured social skills groups. In some cases, it may also be helpful to provide social skills training to parents and caregivers, as they can play an important role in supporting social development.

Early intervention programs can also be helpful for supporting early development in children with ASD. These programs typically involve a multidisciplinary team of professionals, such as speech-language pathologists, occupational therapists, and behavior analysts, who work together to develop an individualized treatment plan for the child. Early intervention programs may include a variety of strategies, such as social skills training, play therapy, speech and language therapy, and behavior intervention.

In addition to these strategies, it is also important for parents, caregivers, and educators to take care of themselves. Caring for a child with ASD can be challenging and stressful, so it is important to practice self-care and seek support when needed. This might include taking breaks when needed, seeking out support groups or counseling, and engaging in activities that promote relaxation and stress reduction.

Chapter Thirteen

The Role of Diet and Nutrition in Autism

Autism spectrum disorder (ASD) is a complex neurodevelopmental condition that affects communication, social interaction, and behavior. While there is no known cure for autism, many treatments and interventions have been developed to help individuals with ASD manage their symptoms and improve their quality of life. One approach that has gained significant attention in recent years is the role of diet and nutrition in autism.

There is no one-size-fits-all diet for individuals with autism, as each person's nutritional needs and sensitivities may vary. However, research has shown that certain dietary changes can have a positive impact on the symptoms of autism.

One of the most commonly studied dietary interventions for autism is the gluten-free, casein-free (GFCF) diet. This diet involves eliminating foods containing gluten, a protein found in wheat, and casein, a protein found in milk and other dairy products. Some studies have suggested that this diet can improve the behavior and communication skills of individuals with autism, although results have been mixed.

Another dietary intervention that has been explored in relation to autism is the ketogenic diet, which is a high-fat, low-carbohydrate diet that puts the body into a state of ketosis. Ketosis has been shown to have therapeutic effects for certain neurological conditions, including epilepsy, and there is some evidence to suggest that it may also be beneficial for individuals with autism. One study found that the ketogenic diet improved the social behavior and cognitive functioning of children with ASD.

In addition to specific dietary interventions, ensuring that individuals with autism are getting adequate levels of key nutrients is also important. Some research has suggested that individuals with autism may have deficiencies in certain vitamins and minerals, including vitamin D, magnesium, and zinc. Supplementing with these nutrients may help to improve the symptoms of autism.

It is also important to consider potential food sensitivities and intolerances in individuals with autism. Some studies have suggested that individuals with autism may be more likely to have food allergies or intolerances, which can exacerbate their symptoms. Identifying and eliminating these problem foods can help to improve overall health and well-being.

While dietary interventions can be helpful for some individuals with autism, it is important to approach these interventions with caution and under the guidance of a healthcare professional. Changes to diet and nutrition should always be made in conjunction with other interventions and therapies, and in consideration of the individual's unique needs and sensitivities.

In addition to dietary interventions, there are other strategies for supporting early development in individuals with autism. Early intervention programs, such as speech therapy, occupational therapy, and behavior therapy, can help to address specific challenges and improve overall functioning. These interventions are often most effective when implemented early, before the age of 3, when the brain is most adaptable.

Strategies for supporting early development may also include sensory integration therapy, which aims to help individuals with autism regulate their sensory experiences and improve their ability to process and respond to sensory input. Sensory integration therapy may involve activities such as swinging, bouncing, and playing in sensory-rich environments.

Other strategies for supporting early development in individuals with autism may include incorporating technology and assistive devices into daily life. Mobile applications and tools designed specifically for individuals with autism can help to support communication, social interaction, and learning.

Common Dietary Interventions for Autism

Autism spectrum disorder (ASD) is a developmental disorder that affects communication, social interaction, and behavior. Many parents and caregivers of individuals with ASD have turned to dietary interventions as a way to improve their symptoms. While there is no cure for ASD, certain diets have been reported to help alleviate some of the symptoms associated with the disorder.

One of the most popular dietary interventions for individuals with ASD is the gluten-free and casein-free (GFCF) diet. This diet involves the elimination of all foods that contain gluten, which is a protein found in wheat, barley, and rye, and casein, which is a protein found in dairy products. The theory behind the GFCF diet is that individuals with ASD have an inability to properly digest these proteins, leading to an increase in the production of opiate-like peptides that can affect behavior and cognitive function. Proponents of the GFCF diet claim that eliminating these proteins from the diet can improve communication, social skills, and behavior in individuals with ASD.

Another popular dietary intervention is the ketogenic diet, which is a high-fat, low-carbohydrate diet that has been used to treat epilepsy. Some studies have suggested that the ketogenic diet may also be beneficial for individuals with ASD, as it has been shown to improve cognitive function and reduce seizures. The theory behind the ketogenic diet is that it can reduce inflammation in the brain, which is believed to be a contributing factor in the development of ASD.

The Specific Carbohydrate Diet (SCD) is another dietary intervention that has gained popularity in the ASD community. The SCD involves the elimination of all grains, sugars, and processed foods, and focuses on the consumption of fruits, vegetables, meats, and nuts. The theory behind the SCD is that many individuals with ASD have an overgrowth of harmful bacteria in their gut, which can lead to inflammation and contribute to the development of ASD symptoms. By eliminating certain foods from the diet and focusing on whole, nutrient-dense foods, the SCD aims to improve gut health and reduce inflammation in the body.

While dietary interventions for ASD have become increasingly popular, it is important to note that there is limited scientific evidence to support their effectiveness. Many studies have been small and not well-controlled, and there is a lack of consensus on which diets are the most effective for improving ASD symptoms. Additionally, some dietary interventions can be difficult to follow and may lead to nutritional deficiencies if not properly balanced.

Despite the lack of scientific evidence, many parents and caregivers of individuals with ASD have reported improvements in their symptoms after implementing dietary interventions. It is important for individuals considering a dietary intervention to speak with a healthcare professional and a registered dietitian to ensure that the diet is safe, nutritionally balanced, and appropriate for the individual's specific needs.

Managing Picky Eating and Sensory Issues

Autism spectrum disorder (ASD) is a complex developmental disorder that affects social communication and behavior. One of the common challenges that individuals with ASD face is related to their eating habits and sensory issues. For some individuals with ASD, food textures, smells, and tastes can be overwhelming, leading to picky eating habits and nutritional deficiencies. Managing picky eating and sensory issues is crucial to ensure that individuals with ASD receive a balanced diet to maintain their overall health and well-being.

The following are some strategies that can be helpful for managing picky eating and sensory issues in individuals with ASD:

1. Understanding sensory issues: Many individuals with ASD have sensory processing issues, which can affect how they perceive and respond to food. Sensory issues can cause individuals with ASD to have aversions to certain textures, smells, and tastes. They may also have a preference for certain types of food. Understanding the sensory preferences and aversions can help identify the types of food that are better accepted and the ones that should be avoided.

2. Introducing new foods gradually: Introducing new foods gradually can help individuals with ASD develop a tolerance for new textures, smells, and tastes. For example, if an individual has an aversion to the texture of vegetables, they can start with introducing small amounts of mashed or pureed vegetables and gradually increase the amount and texture over time.

3. Making food visually appealing: Many individuals with ASD respond well to visual cues. Presenting food in a visually appealing manner can help encourage them to try new foods. Using a colorful plate, arranging food in a visually appealing way, and using fun utensils can make mealtime more appealing.

4. Offering preferred food along with new food: Offering preferred food along with new food can help encourage individuals with ASD to try new foods. For example, if an individual prefers crackers, offering crackers along with a new food can help encourage them to try the new food.

5. Providing a safe environment: Individuals with ASD may feel overwhelmed during mealtimes, leading to food refusal or picky eating. Providing a safe and comfortable environment can help reduce anxiety and make mealtime less stressful. Dimming the lights, playing calming music, or providing a comfortable chair can make the environment more comfortable and conducive to eating.

6. Consulting a registered dietitian: Consulting a registered dietitian can be helpful in identifying nutritional deficiencies and developing a meal plan that meets the individual's nutritional needs. A dietitian can also provide guidance on dietary supplements if needed.

In addition to the above strategies, it is important to involve the individual with ASD in meal planning and preparation. Involving them in meal planning and preparation can help develop an interest in food and increase their willingness to try new foods. It can also be a fun and engaging activity that can help improve their social skills.

Supplements and Nutrient Deficiencies

Supplements and nutrient deficiencies have been an area of interest in the treatment of autism spectrum disorder (ASD). There is evidence that individuals with ASD may have some unique nutrient deficiencies that can be corrected with the use of supplements. Below we will explore the relationship between supplements and nutrient deficiencies in individuals with ASD.

It is important to note that while some studies have suggested that certain supplements may be beneficial for individuals with ASD, there is currently no one-size-fits-all approach to supplement use. Each individual with ASD is unique, and it is important to work with a healthcare provider to determine which supplements may be beneficial.

One of the nutrients that has been of interest in the treatment of ASD is omega-3 fatty acids. Omega-3 fatty acids are important for brain function, and studies have suggested that individuals with ASD may have lower levels of omega-3 fatty acids than their typically developing peers. Several studies have suggested that supplementation with omega-3 fatty acids may improve some symptoms of ASD, such as hyperactivity, social interaction, and cognitive function. However, not all studies have shown a significant effect of omega-3 fatty acid supplementation, and more research is needed to determine if it is a helpful supplement for individuals with ASD.

Another nutrient that has been of interest is vitamin D. Vitamin D is important for bone health and immune function, and some studies have suggested that individuals with ASD may have lower levels of vitamin D than their typically developing peers. Some studies have suggested that supplementation with vitamin D may improve some symptoms of ASD, such as irritability and social withdrawal. However, more research is needed to determine if vitamin D is a helpful supplement for individuals with ASD.

Probiotics are another supplement that has been of interest in the treatment of ASD. Probiotics are beneficial bacteria that are found in the gut, and some studies have suggested that individuals with ASD may have an imbalance of gut bacteria. Some studies have suggested that supplementation with probiotics may improve some symptoms of ASD, such as gastrointestinal symptoms and irritability. However, more research is needed to determine if probiotics are a helpful supplement for individuals with ASD.

While supplements may be beneficial for some individuals with ASD, it is important to note that they should not be used as a replacement for a healthy diet. It is important for individuals with ASD to consume a well-balanced diet that includes a variety of nutrient-rich foods.

In addition to supplements, nutrient deficiencies have also been of interest in the treatment of ASD. Some studies have suggested that individuals with ASD may have lower levels of certain nutrients, such as zinc and magnesium, than their typically developing peers. Correcting these nutrient deficiencies with the use of supplements or dietary changes may improve some symptoms of ASD, such as irritability and hyperactivity.

It is important to note that while supplements and nutrient deficiencies have been of interest in the treatment of ASD, more research is needed to determine their effectiveness. It is also important to work with a healthcare provider to determine which supplements and dietary changes may be beneficial, as each individual with ASD is unique and may have different needs.

Chapter Fourteen

Autism and Physical Activity

Autism spectrum disorder (ASD) is a developmental disorder that affects a person's ability to communicate and interact with others. Individuals with autism may also experience difficulties with sensory processing, behavior, and cognition. Physical activity has been shown to have positive effects on many of the challenges faced by individuals with autism. Below we will explore the benefits of physical activity for people with autism and the strategies for incorporating it into their daily lives.

Physical activity has many benefits for individuals with autism. It can improve mood, decrease anxiety, and reduce repetitive behaviors. Additionally, physical activity can help with the development of gross motor skills and coordination, which are often delayed in individuals with autism. Studies have also shown that physical activity can improve social skills, such as turn-taking and sharing.

There are many different types of physical activities that can be beneficial for individuals with autism. These include individual activities such as swimming, running, and cycling, as well as team sports like basketball, soccer, and baseball. Martial arts and yoga have also been found to be helpful for individuals with autism because they promote balance, flexibility, and focus.

In order to successfully incorporate physical activity into the lives of individuals with autism, it is important to consider their unique needs and challenges. For example, individuals with sensory processing issues may find certain types of physical activities overwhelming or uncomfortable. In this case, it may be helpful to gradually introduce activities and provide sensory supports such as weighted vests or earplugs.

It is also important to consider the individual's interests and preferences when choosing physical activities. Some individuals with autism may prefer solo activities like swimming or running, while others may thrive in team sports that provide social interaction and a sense of community. By incorporating activities that the individual enjoys, they are more likely to stick with it and reap the benefits.

Another important consideration is the environment in which physical activity takes place. Individuals with autism may have difficulty with transitions and changes in routine, so it is important to create a consistent and predictable environment for physical activity. This may involve using the same space for physical activity each time, providing clear instructions, and using visual schedules or timers to help with transitions.

In addition to individual physical activities, group physical activity programs can be a great way to promote physical fitness and social interaction for individuals with autism. These programs are often led by trained professionals who understand the unique needs and challenges of individuals with autism. Some examples of group physical activity programs for individuals with autism include Special Olympics, Miracle League baseball, and Best Buddies.

The Benefits of Exercise for Individuals with Autism

Autism Spectrum Disorder (ASD) is a neurodevelopmental disorder that affects communication, social interaction, and behavior. One of the challenges that individuals with autism face is finding activities that they enjoy and can participate in comfortably. However, physical activity and exercise have been found to have numerous benefits for individuals with autism, including improving physical health, social skills, behavior, and reducing stress and anxiety.

Physical activity has a positive impact on physical health, such as improving cardiovascular health, muscular strength, and motor skills. Studies have shown that individuals with autism tend to have lower physical fitness levels than their neurotypical peers. Physical activity can help improve these fitness levels and reduce the risk of obesity and other health problems. Additionally, regular exercise has been found to improve sleep quality and promote better sleep hygiene, which can improve overall health and wellbeing.

In addition to physical health benefits, exercise can also help improve social skills and behavior in individuals with autism. Many individuals with autism struggle with social skills and can benefit from social interaction in a structured setting. Participating in group activities, such as sports or fitness classes, can help individuals with autism learn to interact with others and develop positive relationships. Exercise can also help improve behavior by reducing hyperactivity, aggression, and stereotypical behaviors.

Exercise is also an effective way to reduce stress and anxiety in individuals with autism. Many individuals with autism experience high levels of stress and anxiety, which can be difficult to manage. Regular exercise has been found to reduce stress and anxiety levels by increasing the production of endorphins, which are natural mood-boosters. Exercise can also provide a structured and predictable routine, which can help individuals with autism feel more comfortable and secure.

There are several types of physical activities and exercises that can be beneficial for individuals with autism. Aerobic exercise, such as running or cycling, can improve cardiovascular health and promote overall fitness.

Strength training exercises, such as lifting weights, can help improve muscular strength and balance. Yoga and other mindfulness-based practices can help improve flexibility, balance, and relaxation.

It is important to note that some individuals with autism may have sensory issues that make certain types of physical activities and exercises uncomfortable or overwhelming. For example, some individuals may be sensitive to loud noises, bright lights, or certain textures. It is important to work with a healthcare provider or therapist to identify appropriate activities and make any necessary accommodations.

Adapting Sports and Physical Activities for Autism

Adapting sports and physical activities for individuals with autism can provide many benefits, including improving social skills, enhancing physical fitness, and reducing stress and anxiety. However, traditional sports and activities may not be suitable for all individuals with autism, as they may have difficulty with sensory processing, communication, and social interactions. Therefore, it is important to understand how to adapt sports and physical activities to meet the needs of individuals with autism.

One important consideration when adapting sports and physical activities is sensory processing. Individuals with autism may be hypersensitive or hyposensitive to certain sensory stimuli, such as touch, sound, and movement. This can make it difficult to participate in sports and physical activities that involve these types of sensory input. For example, some individuals with autism may be overwhelmed by the noise and activity of a crowded gym or sports field. Others may have difficulty with the sensation of certain fabrics or equipment. To address these challenges, it may be helpful to provide accommodations such as noise-cancelling headphones, weighted vests, or sensory-friendly equipment.

Another consideration when adapting sports and physical activities is communication. Many individuals with autism have difficulty with communication, which can make it challenging to follow directions or understand the rules of a game. It is important to use clear, concise language and provide visual aids whenever possible. For example, using picture schedules or visual cue cards can help individuals with autism understand what they are supposed to do and when.

Social interactions can also be challenging for individuals with autism, and this can impact their participation in sports and physical activities. Traditional team sports may be overwhelming or anxiety-provoking for some individuals with autism, as they may struggle with the complex social rules and expectations that come with team sports. However, there are many other physical activities that can provide social opportunities in a less overwhelming setting. For example, yoga, martial arts, or swimming classes can provide opportunities for social interaction in a smaller, more structured environment.

Adapting sports and physical activities for individuals with autism can also involve modifying the goals and expectations of the activity. For example, some individuals with autism may have difficulty with coordination or balance, which can make it difficult to participate in certain sports. Modifying the rules or expectations of the activity can help these individuals feel successful and included. For example, instead of requiring an individual to catch a ball, they could be asked to hold the ball for a certain amount of time or pass it to another player.

It is also important to consider the individual's interests and strengths when adapting sports and physical activities. Some individuals with autism may have a particular interest in a certain sport or activity, such as swimming or running. Finding ways to incorporate these interests into physical activities can increase motivation and engagement. Additionally, some individuals with autism may have strengths in certain areas, such as flexibility or strength. Modifying activities to highlight these strengths can increase feelings of competence and success.

Building Motor Skills and Coordination

Building Motor Skills and Coordination in Individuals with Autism

Autism is a developmental disorder that affects communication, social interaction, and behavior. One area that can be impacted by autism is motor skills and coordination. Individuals with autism may experience delays or difficulties in developing gross and fine motor skills, which can impact their ability to engage in daily activities and participate in physical play and sports. However, with the right support and interventions, individuals with autism can improve their motor skills and coordination and enjoy the benefits of physical activity and play.

Gross motor skills are the abilities to control large muscles that allow for movement of the body, such as crawling, walking, jumping, and running. Fine motor skills are the abilities to control small muscles that allow for movement of the hands and fingers, such as grasping, writing, and drawing. Both gross and fine motor skills are important for daily activities, such as dressing, eating, and writing.

Many children with autism experience delays in the development of gross and fine motor skills. This can be due to a variety of factors, including differences in brain development and sensory processing. For example, some children with autism may have difficulty with balance and coordination, which can make it challenging to participate in physical activities that require these skills. Other children with autism may have difficulty with hand-eye coordination and fine motor skills, which can impact their ability to write, draw, and perform other tasks that require hand dexterity and control.

Fortunately, there are many interventions and strategies that can help individuals with autism improve their motor skills and coordination. One approach that has been shown to be effective is physical therapy. Physical therapy can help children with autism develop strength, coordination, and balance through targeted exercises and activities. A physical therapist can work with the child to develop a personalized plan that addresses their specific needs and challenges.

Occupational therapy is another intervention that can be helpful for improving motor skills and coordination in individuals with autism. Occupational therapists focus on developing the skills needed for daily living and work, such as fine motor skills, self-care, and sensory processing. An occupational therapist can work with the child to develop activities and exercises that help them improve their motor skills and coordination while also addressing other areas of development.

In addition to therapy, there are many other strategies that can be used to help individuals with autism develop their motor skills and coordination. For example, structured play activities can be helpful in developing gross motor skills, such as jumping and running. These activities can be tailored to the child's interests and abilities to make them engaging and enjoyable. Fine motor skills can be developed through activities such as drawing, painting, and using manipulatives like playdough or building blocks.

It is also important to consider the sensory needs of individuals with autism when designing activities to improve motor skills and coordination. Many individuals with autism have sensory processing differences that can impact their ability to participate in physical activities. For example, some may be hypersensitive to certain textures or sounds, while others may seek out sensory input through movement or touch. By understanding an individual's sensory needs, caregivers and therapists can develop activities that are appropriate and enjoyable for the individual.

In addition to improving motor skills and coordination, physical activity and play can have many other benefits for individuals with autism. Engaging in physical activity can help improve mood, reduce anxiety, and increase self-esteem. It can also provide opportunities for social interaction and communication, which can be challenging for some individuals with autism. Participating in team sports or other physical activities can provide opportunities for individuals with autism to develop social skills and make friends.

Chapter Fifteen

Creativity and the Arts in Autism

Creativity and the arts have always been recognized as a way for individuals to express themselves, connect with others, and explore their own thoughts and feelings. For individuals with autism, the arts have proven to be a valuable tool for communication and self-expression. Below we will explore the various ways in which creativity and the arts can benefit individuals with autism.

One of the most commonly recognized benefits of the arts for individuals with autism is the ability to communicate thoughts and feelings that may be difficult to express through traditional communication methods. Many individuals with autism struggle with verbal communication, and the arts provide an alternative means of expression. Through music, art, and other creative outlets, individuals with autism can express themselves in ways that they may not be able to do with words.

In addition to providing an alternative means of communication, the arts also offer individuals with autism an opportunity to explore their own thoughts and emotions. Many individuals with autism struggle with identifying and understanding their own emotions, which can lead to frustration and isolation. By engaging in creative activities, individuals with autism can learn to identify and express their emotions, which can help them to better understand themselves and the world around them.

The arts also offer a way for individuals with autism to connect with others. Many individuals with autism struggle with social interactions, and the arts provide a way for them to connect with others in a non-threatening and non-judgmental environment. Through participation in group activities such as music or drama, individuals with autism can learn to interact with others in a positive and supportive environment.

Music is a particularly powerful tool for individuals with autism. Research has shown that music can help to reduce anxiety, improve social skills, and enhance communication abilities in individuals with autism. Music therapy, which involves the use of music to achieve therapeutic goals, has become an increasingly popular treatment option for individuals with autism. Music therapy sessions can include activities such as singing, playing instruments, and listening to music, all of which have been shown to be effective in improving social skills, communication, and overall well-being in individuals with autism.

Art therapy is another popular treatment option for individuals with autism. Art therapy involves the use of art to promote emotional, cognitive, and social growth. Through activities such as painting, drawing, and sculpting, individuals with autism can express themselves and explore their own emotions in a safe and supportive environment. Art therapy has been shown to be effective in improving social skills, reducing anxiety, and enhancing overall well-being in individuals with autism.

Drama therapy is another creative treatment option that has been shown to be effective in improving social skills and communication in individuals with autism. Drama therapy involves the use of role-playing and improvisation to explore social situations and practice communication skills. Through drama therapy, individuals with autism can learn to interact with others in a positive and supportive environment, which can help to improve their overall social skills and communication abilities.

In addition to the therapeutic benefits of the arts, creative activities such as music, art, and drama also offer individuals with autism an opportunity to develop new skills and interests. Many individuals with autism have a special talent or passion for the arts, and engaging in creative activities can help to foster and develop these interests. By participating in music lessons, art classes, or drama clubs, individuals with autism can develop new skills and explore their own interests in a supportive and non-judgmental environment.

Music Therapy and Its Benefits

Music therapy is a well-known approach that uses music to achieve therapeutic goals. It is a valuable resource for individuals with autism who may have difficulty communicating or expressing themselves in traditional ways. Music therapy uses various techniques to address physical, emotional, cognitive, and social needs and improve overall well-being.

Music therapy has been shown to improve social interaction skills, communication, motor skills, and cognitive abilities in individuals with autism. For example, playing an instrument or singing in a group can help develop social skills such as taking turns, sharing, and cooperation. Music can also be used as a tool to improve communication skills, by singing along to a song, and learning to articulate lyrics.

Music therapy can also help to improve motor skills and coordination. Some techniques used in music therapy include using instruments such as drums, percussion, and xylophones to promote hand-eye coordination, finger dexterity, and body movement. Playing an instrument can also help to develop fine motor skills, while dancing or moving to the beat can promote gross motor skills.

One of the most significant benefits of music therapy is its ability to reduce anxiety and promote relaxation. Music can be used as a coping mechanism to manage anxiety or stress, and it can be especially beneficial for individuals with autism who may have difficulty communicating their feelings. Music can also help to regulate emotions and promote emotional expression.

Music therapy is a highly adaptable treatment approach, and can be customized to meet the specific needs of each individual. Music therapists work closely with individuals with autism to develop individualized treatment plans, tailored to their unique needs and goals.

There are several different approaches to music therapy, including receptive and active methods. Receptive music therapy involves listening to music, while active music therapy involves participating in music-making activities such as playing an instrument or singing. Both approaches can be used to achieve therapeutic goals, and therapists often use a combination of techniques to achieve the best results.

Music therapy can be used in a variety of settings, including schools, hospitals, and community centers. Many music therapists work in collaboration with other healthcare professionals to provide comprehensive care to individuals with autism.

In addition to its therapeutic benefits, music therapy can also be a fun and engaging activity that promotes creativity and self-expression. Music can be a powerful tool for individuals with autism to express themselves and connect with others.

While music therapy has many benefits, it is important to note that it is not a cure for autism. Rather, it is one of many tools that can be used to improve the overall well-being of individuals with autism. Additionally, music therapy may not be suitable for everyone with autism, and it is important to work with a qualified music therapist to determine whether it is the right approach for each individual.

Art and Creative Expression for Individuals with Autism

Art and creative expression can be powerful tools for individuals with autism. They offer a way to communicate thoughts and feelings that may be difficult to express verbally, and can provide a way to develop social skills, fine motor skills, and emotional regulation. Below we will explore the benefits of art and creative expression for individuals with autism and how it can be used as a form of therapy.

One of the primary benefits of art and creative expression for individuals with autism is the ability to communicate and express themselves in a nonverbal way. Many individuals with autism struggle with verbal communication, and art can provide a way to express their thoughts and emotions in a way that is comfortable for them. Art can also provide a way to process sensory information and help individuals with autism make sense of their environment.

In addition to communication, art can also provide a way to develop fine motor skills. Many individuals with autism struggle with fine motor skills and may have difficulty with tasks such as writing or cutting with scissors. Art can provide a fun and engaging way to practice these skills and develop new ones.

Art can also be used to develop social skills. Group art activities can provide an opportunity for individuals with autism to practice social interaction, turn-taking, and collaboration. Art can also provide a way to develop empathy and understanding for others, as individuals with autism can create art that represents the perspective of others.

One specific form of therapy that utilizes art is art therapy. Art therapy is a form of psychotherapy that uses art as a way to help individuals express their emotions, improve communication, and develop self-awareness. Art therapists work with individuals to help them create art that represents their thoughts and feelings, and then use the art as a starting point for discussion and exploration.

Art therapy can be particularly effective for individuals with autism, as it provides a way to communicate and process emotions in a nonverbal way. Art therapists can also help individuals with autism develop coping skills and emotional regulation through art. For example, an individual with autism may create a painting to represent their feelings of anger, and then work with the therapist to develop strategies for managing those feelings in a constructive way.

Another form of therapy that utilizes art is music therapy. Music therapy is a form of therapy that uses music as a way to promote physical, emotional, cognitive, and social well-being. Music therapists work with individuals to create music that is tailored to their specific needs and goals.

Music therapy can be particularly effective for individuals with autism, as it provides a way to engage with others and develop social skills through shared musical experiences. Music can also provide a way to process sensory information and improve emotional regulation. For example, an individual with autism may listen to calming music to help regulate their emotions during a stressful situation.

In addition to therapy, art and creative expression can also provide a way to engage with the world and develop a sense of identity. Many individuals with autism have interests or talents in areas such as art, music, or writing. Pursuing these interests can provide a sense of purpose and meaning in life, and can also provide a way to connect with others who share similar interests.

The Role of Drama and Theatre in Building Social Skills

The performing arts have been found to be a highly effective tool in helping individuals with autism develop social skills, communication, and self-expression. Drama and theater are especially beneficial in this regard, as they provide a safe and structured environment in which individuals with autism can explore social situations and emotions.

One of the main advantages of drama and theater for individuals with autism is that it provides a structured and predictable environment. People with autism often have difficulty with unstructured or unpredictable situations, as they prefer routine and consistency. In drama and theater, there are clear rules and expectations that provide a sense of structure and stability. This can help individuals with autism feel more comfortable and secure, which can in turn improve their ability to participate and engage with others.

Another advantage of drama and theater for individuals with autism is that it provides a safe space in which to practice social interactions. In a drama or theater class, participants are given the opportunity to explore and practice different social scenarios, such as introducing themselves, making eye contact, and engaging in conversation. These scenarios can be rehearsed in a safe and supportive environment, which can help individuals with autism feel more confident and comfortable in social situations.

Drama and theater also provide a unique opportunity for individuals with autism to express themselves creatively. Many people with autism have a strong affinity for the arts, and may be highly skilled in areas such as music, drawing, or acting. By participating in drama and theater classes, individuals with autism are able to use these skills to express themselves and communicate with others. This can be especially important for individuals with autism who struggle with verbal communication or who find it difficult to express their emotions.

In addition to these benefits, drama and theater can also improve a number of other skills and abilities in individuals with autism. For example, research has shown that drama and theater can improve nonverbal communication skills, such as facial expressions and body language. It can also improve self-regulation and impulse control, as participants learn to control their emotions and behavior in response to different social situations.

To be effective, drama and theater programs for individuals with autism should be designed with their unique needs and abilities in mind. Teachers and facilitators should have a strong understanding of autism and its associated challenges, and should be trained in techniques for working with individuals with autism. They should also be able to adapt the curriculum and activities to suit the needs of individual participants, taking into account factors such as sensory sensitivities, communication abilities, and social preferences.

Chapter Sixteen

Autism Around the World

Autism is a complex neurodevelopmental disorder that affects communication, social interaction, and behavior. It is a global phenomenon, with estimates of prevalence ranging from 1 in 100 to 1 in 300 individuals worldwide. While there is no known cure for autism, early diagnosis and intervention can make a significant difference in improving the quality of life for individuals with autism.

The experience of autism varies widely across cultures and countries. In some cultures, social norms and expectations may be more or less accommodating to the unique needs and challenges of individuals with autism. This can lead to differences in how autism is understood and approached in different parts of the world.

In Western cultures, autism is typically diagnosed through the use of standardized diagnostic tools and criteria, such as the DSM-5. The focus is often on identifying deficits in social communication and interaction, as well as the presence of repetitive behaviors and restricted interests. Early intervention services may include behavioral therapies, speech and language therapy, and occupational therapy.

In other cultures, however, autism may be understood and treated differently. For example, in some parts of Asia, there may be less emphasis on individual diagnosis and more focus on the family unit. In such cases, families may seek out support and guidance from community members and traditional healers rather than formal medical professionals.

In some cultures, there may also be different expectations regarding social interaction and communication. For instance, in some parts of Africa, nonverbal communication and physical touch may be more highly valued and emphasized than in Western cultures. This can present unique challenges for individuals with autism, who may struggle with nonverbal communication and touch sensitivity.

Despite these cultural differences, many of the challenges faced by individuals with autism are universal. In all cultures, individuals with autism may struggle to form and maintain social relationships, communicate effectively, and adapt to changes in routine or environment. They may also experience sensory sensitivities and other co-occurring conditions, such as anxiety and depression.

One area of particular concern in autism around the world is access to services and support. In many parts of the world, there may be limited resources and funding for autism research, diagnosis, and treatment. This can lead to long wait times for services and a lack of adequate support for individuals with autism and their families.

Additionally, cultural stigma and misinformation surrounding autism can make it difficult for families to seek out and access services. In some cultures, autism may be viewed as a form of punishment or shame, leading to feelings of isolation and exclusion.

Despite these challenges, there are many organizations and initiatives working to increase awareness and support for individuals with autism around the world. International autism conferences and networks provide opportunities for collaboration and knowledge sharing among professionals and advocates. Local and national advocacy groups work to promote greater understanding and acceptance of autism, as well as access to services and support.

As the understanding of autism continues to evolve, it is important to recognize the unique experiences and challenges faced by individuals with autism in different cultures and countries. By promoting greater awareness and understanding of autism around the world, we can work towards a more inclusive and supportive global community for individuals with autism and their families.

Cultural Perspectives on Autism

Autism is a neurodevelopmental disorder that affects individuals across cultures, races, and ethnicities. However, the way autism is perceived and treated can vary widely across different cultures. Cultural factors can influence how families view autism, how individuals with autism are diagnosed and treated, and how society at large perceives and responds to individuals with autism.

In many cultures, there is a stigma attached to developmental disabilities, including autism. Families may feel ashamed or embarrassed to have a child with autism and may be hesitant to seek out support or treatment. This can be especially true in countries where disability is seen as a punishment for wrongdoing or as a result of a lack of faith or spiritual alignment.

In some cultures, there may also be a lack of awareness or understanding of autism. For example, in many African countries, there is a common belief that developmental disabilities are caused by witchcraft or a curse, rather than by biological factors. As a result, families may seek out traditional healers or spiritual leaders rather than medical professionals for treatment.

The way autism is diagnosed and treated can also vary across cultures. In some countries, there may be a lack of access to diagnostic tools or specialized professionals who can diagnose autism. In other countries, there may be cultural biases that can affect the diagnostic process. For example, in some cultures, shyness or social withdrawal may be seen as a sign of politeness or respect, rather than as a symptom of a developmental disorder like autism.

Treatment options for autism can also vary depending on cultural factors. Some families may be more comfortable with traditional or alternative treatments, such as herbal remedies or acupuncture, rather than medical interventions. In some cultures, there may also be a preference for group therapies or interventions that involve the entire family, rather than individualized treatment plans.

Despite these differences, there is also a growing recognition of the importance of supporting individuals with autism across cultures. In many countries, advocacy groups and support networks are working to increase awareness and understanding of autism and to promote more inclusive policies and practices. There are also efforts to develop culturally sensitive diagnostic tools and treatment approaches that take into account the unique needs and perspectives of individuals and families from different cultures.

One area where cultural perspectives on autism can have a particularly significant impact is in education. In some cultures, there may be a greater emphasis on conformity and obedience, which can make it challenging for individuals with autism to thrive in traditional classroom settings. However, there are also many examples of successful educational programs that have been adapted to meet the needs of individuals with autism from diverse cultural backgrounds.

For example, in Japan, there is a strong emphasis on group harmony and social conformity. However, there are also innovative programs that have been developed to help children with autism to learn in small, structured groups that emphasize individualized attention and support. In India, where there is a high value placed on spiritual and emotional development, there are schools that use yoga and meditation as a part of their curriculum to help students with autism to develop self-regulation and social skills.

International Approaches to Autism Treatment and Support

Autism is a global issue affecting individuals and families across the world. As such, different countries have developed their own approaches to autism treatment and support. Below we will explore some of the international approaches to autism treatment and support.

In the United States, the most commonly used approach to autism treatment is Applied Behavior Analysis (ABA). ABA focuses on using positive reinforcement to shape behaviors and teach new skills. This approach is widely recognized and has been endorsed by organizations such as the American Academy of Pediatrics and the National Institutes of Health. In addition to ABA, many children with autism in the United States receive occupational, speech, and physical therapy.

In Canada, the approach to autism treatment and support is more varied, with a focus on individualized interventions. While ABA is also used in Canada, there is also an emphasis on sensory integration therapy, which focuses on addressing sensory processing issues. Other approaches used in Canada include social skills training, play-based therapy, and parent training programs.

In Europe, there is a growing emphasis on holistic, multidisciplinary approaches to autism treatment and support. Many countries in Europe use a combination of interventions, including speech and language therapy, occupational therapy, and behavioral interventions. In addition, many European countries have developed programs to support adults with autism, including vocational training and job coaching.

In Asia, autism is often viewed through a cultural lens, with a focus on the collective well-being of the family and community. As such, there is often a greater emphasis on family-based interventions and support, as well as a focus on social skills and communication. In Japan, for example, there is a focus on group-based interventions, including group therapy and social skills training. In China, there is a focus on integrating children with autism into mainstream classrooms.

In Australia, there is a focus on early intervention and evidence-based approaches to autism treatment and support. Like Canada, there is an emphasis on individualized interventions, with a focus on addressing sensory processing issues and promoting social communication skills. In addition, many children with autism in Australia receive speech and language therapy, occupational therapy, and behavioral interventions.

In Africa, access to autism treatment and support can be more limited due to a lack of resources and awareness. However, there are some programs and organizations working to address this issue. In South Africa, for example, there is a growing movement to increase awareness of autism and improve access to services. In Kenya, there is a program called Autism Support Kenya that provides training and support to families and professionals.

In the Middle East, there is a growing interest in autism treatment and support. However, there can be cultural barriers to accessing services, as well as a lack of resources. In Israel, for example, there is a focus on early intervention and parent training programs. In Saudi Arabia, there is a growing interest in using technology-based interventions, such as teletherapy.

Global Autism Awareness and Advocacy Efforts

Autism is a neurological condition that affects individuals worldwide. While the prevalence rates and diagnostic criteria may vary across cultures and regions, the experiences of individuals and families affected by autism share similarities. Therefore, global awareness and advocacy efforts are crucial to improving the lives of individuals with autism and their families. Below we will discuss the global efforts in autism awareness and advocacy.

Autism awareness and advocacy efforts have gained momentum over the years, with organizations and individuals working towards improving the lives of those affected by autism. The United Nations has recognized April 2nd as World Autism Awareness Day since 2008, which has led to a global campaign to increase awareness about autism. This day is observed globally with various events and activities aimed at promoting awareness about autism and improving the lives of individuals and families affected by autism. For instance, in some countries, buildings and monuments are lit up in blue, which is the color representing autism awareness, while others organize fundraising events to support autism research and services.

The World Health Organization (WHO) has recognized autism as a global public health priority, which has led to the development of autism initiatives and action plans in several countries. The WHO has also published the "World Report on Disability," which includes autism as a major disability, emphasizing the need for support and inclusion of individuals with autism in all aspects of society. Furthermore, the WHO has published guidelines for early identification and intervention of autism, which can help families and professionals in different countries to identify and support individuals with autism.

International organizations such as Autism Speaks and the International Society for Autism Research (INSAR) have played significant roles in increasing autism awareness and supporting research worldwide. Autism Speaks has a global presence, with offices in several countries, and provides resources and support for families affected by autism. INSAR organizes annual international conferences on autism research, which bring together researchers and professionals from around the world to share their knowledge and advancements in autism research.

In addition to organizations, many individuals are working to promote autism awareness and advocacy worldwide. For instance, in India, Arman Ali founded the Autism Centre for Excellence (ACE) to provide support and services for individuals with autism and their families. In Nigeria, Oluwatoyin Sanni founded the Autism Parents Association to raise awareness about autism and provide support for families affected by autism. These are just a few examples of individuals making a difference in their countries and communities.

Despite the progress made in autism awareness and advocacy, there are still significant challenges. Many countries lack adequate resources and support for individuals with autism and their families, leading to stigma, discrimination, and exclusion. Additionally, cultural beliefs and attitudes towards disability can impact the acceptance and inclusion of individuals with autism in different societies. Therefore, efforts to promote awareness and acceptance of autism must take into account cultural and regional differences.

Chapter Seventeen

The Future of Autism Research

Autism is a complex neurodevelopmental disorder that affects communication, social interaction, and behavior. It is estimated that 1 in 54 children in the United States has autism, making it one of the most common developmental disabilities in the country. Despite the growing prevalence of autism, there is still much to be learned about the disorder and its causes. As a result, research on autism is an important area of study that holds the potential for significant advancements in the understanding, diagnosis, and treatment of the disorder.

One area of future research in autism is focused on the identification of genetic and environmental factors that may contribute to the development of the disorder. Although there is a genetic component to autism, the exact genes and interactions that lead to the disorder are not yet fully understood. Additionally, environmental factors such as prenatal exposure to toxins or certain medications may also play a role in the development of autism. Identifying these factors could lead to improved understanding of the disorder and potentially lead to new strategies for prevention or treatment.

Another important area of research in autism is the development of diagnostic tools that can accurately identify individuals with the disorder. Currently, autism is typically diagnosed through observation of behavior and communication patterns, which can be subjective and may lead to missed or incorrect diagnoses. Developing objective diagnostic tools, such as genetic testing or brain imaging, could improve the accuracy of autism diagnosis and help individuals receive appropriate treatment and support.

Research on the effectiveness of autism treatments is also a crucial area of study. Currently, there is no cure for autism, and treatments are focused on managing symptoms and improving quality of life. However, the effectiveness of current treatments, such as behavioral therapy and medication, varies widely among individuals with autism. Continued research on the effectiveness of different treatment approaches and the identification of biomarkers or other predictors of treatment response could lead to more personalized and effective treatments for individuals with autism.

In addition to these specific areas of research, there are also broader efforts to improve the understanding and support of individuals with autism. For example, the concept of neurodiversity, which recognizes that differences in brain function and behavior are a natural part of human variation, has gained increasing attention in recent years. Embracing neurodiversity and understanding the strengths and challenges of individuals with autism can lead to greater acceptance and inclusion in society.

Emerging Research and Understanding of Autism

Autism, or autism spectrum disorder (ASD), is a complex neurodevelopmental condition that affects social communication and interaction, as well as sensory and behavioral patterns. Over the years, research has contributed significantly to our understanding of autism and how it impacts individuals and their families. Emerging research is providing new insights into the condition and the potential for innovative interventions and treatments.

One significant area of research in autism is genetics. Recent studies have identified specific genes that may contribute to the development of autism.

Researchers have identified a range of genetic variations that can increase the risk of developing autism, and these variations may affect the way the brain develops and functions. This research has important implications for early identification and treatment of autism and for understanding the underlying mechanisms of the disorder.

Another area of emerging research is focused on brain development in individuals with autism. Recent studies have used advanced imaging techniques to investigate the structure and function of the brain in individuals with ASD. This research has revealed that individuals with autism show differences in brain connectivity and activity compared to typically developing individuals. This research is providing new insights into the neural basis of autism and how it affects social communication and interaction.

Research is also being conducted on the effectiveness of early intervention programs for children with autism. Early intervention programs aim to provide children with the skills they need to develop social communication and interaction skills, and to minimize the impact of autism on their lives. Recent studies have shown that early intervention programs can significantly improve outcomes for children with autism. These programs typically involve a combination of behavioral and developmental therapies, and may be tailored to meet the specific needs of each individual child.

Researchers are also investigating the potential of technology in the assessment and treatment of autism. For example, virtual reality (VR) technology is being explored as a tool for social skills training in individuals with autism. VR technology can provide a safe and controlled environment for individuals with autism to practice social interaction and communication skills. Other technological tools, such as apps and wearable devices, are also being developed to support individuals with autism and their families.

Finally, research is focused on the co-occurrence of other conditions in individuals with autism, such as anxiety, depression, and sleep disorders. Recent studies have shown that individuals with autism are at a higher risk of developing these conditions compared to the general population. Understanding the co-occurrence of these conditions can help to inform interventions and treatments that may improve outcomes for individuals with autism.

Potential Breakthroughs in Treatment and Intervention

Potential Breakthroughs in Treatment and Intervention for Autism

Autism, or autism spectrum disorder (ASD), is a complex neurodevelopmental disorder that affects social interaction, communication, and behavior. While there is no known cure for autism, there are a variety of treatments and interventions available to help manage symptoms and improve quality of life for individuals with the disorder. In recent years, researchers have been working to identify new breakthroughs in autism treatment and intervention that may provide even more effective options for individuals with autism and their families.

One promising area of research in autism treatment is the development of new medications. Currently, there are only a few medications that have been approved by the U.S. Food and Drug Administration (FDA) to treat some of the symptoms associated with autism, such as irritability and aggression. However, research is ongoing to identify new medications that may be effective in treating other aspects of the disorder, such as social communication difficulties.

Another area of research that shows promise in autism treatment is the use of transcranial magnetic stimulation (TMS). TMS is a non-invasive brain stimulation technique that uses magnetic fields to stimulate nerve cells in the brain. While still in the early stages of research, TMS has shown potential in improving social communication skills and reducing repetitive behaviors in individuals with autism.

Gene therapy is another area of research that holds potential for autism treatment. Researchers have identified several genes that are associated with autism, and are exploring ways to modify or replace these genes in order to improve symptoms. While gene therapy is still in the early stages of research, it has shown promising results in animal studies and may eventually provide a targeted approach to treating autism.

In addition to new medications and therapies, there is also ongoing research into the effectiveness of existing treatments for autism. For example, studies have shown that early intervention programs, such as applied behavior analysis (ABA), can be highly effective in improving social communication skills and reducing problem behaviors in young children with autism. Research is also being conducted to determine the effectiveness of other therapies, such as occupational therapy and speech therapy, in improving outcomes for individuals with autism.

Another promising area of research in autism treatment is the use of technology. Researchers are exploring the potential of virtual reality and other interactive technologies to provide new ways of delivering therapy and improving outcomes for individuals with autism. For example, virtual reality therapy may be used to help individuals with autism practice social interactions in a safe and controlled environment, while other technologies may be used to track and monitor symptoms over time.

In addition to new treatments, there is also a growing focus on improving the understanding of autism and reducing stigma surrounding the disorder. This includes research into the genetic and environmental factors that contribute to autism, as well as efforts to increase public awareness and understanding of the disorder. Some researchers are also exploring the potential of using biomarkers, such as brain imaging and genetic testing, to diagnose autism earlier and provide more targeted treatments.

While there is still much to learn about autism and its treatment, ongoing research is providing new hope for individuals with the disorder and their families. As our understanding of autism continues to evolve, it is likely that new breakthroughs in treatment and intervention will emerge, providing even more effective options for those affected by autism.

The Importance of Continued Research and Funding

Autism is a complex neurodevelopmental disorder that affects individuals differently. It is characterized by impaired social communication and repetitive behaviors and interests. While there is currently no known cure for autism, there are several treatments and interventions available that can help individuals with autism lead fulfilling lives. Research is a crucial aspect of understanding and developing effective treatments for autism. Below we will explore the importance of continued research and funding for autism.

First and foremost, research is essential for understanding the underlying causes of autism. There is currently no known single cause of autism, and it is likely that a combination of genetic and environmental factors contribute to its development. Research can help identify these factors and provide a better understanding of how they interact with each other. By identifying the underlying causes of autism, researchers can develop more targeted and effective treatments for individuals with autism.

Secondly, research is crucial for developing new and effective treatments for autism. While there are several treatments and interventions available, they are not effective for everyone with autism. Continued research can help develop new treatments and interventions that are tailored to individual needs. For example, recent research has shown promising results in the use of stem cells for the treatment of autism. Stem cells can potentially help repair damaged neurons in the brain and improve social communication and cognitive abilities in individuals with autism. Further research in this area could lead to a breakthrough in the treatment of autism.

Additionally, research is important for understanding the long-term outcomes of individuals with autism. Autism is a lifelong condition, and individuals with autism face unique challenges throughout their lives. Understanding the long-term outcomes of individuals with autism is crucial for developing effective support and resources for individuals with autism and their families. Research can help identify the most effective interventions for improving long-term outcomes for individuals with autism.

Furthermore, research is crucial for reducing stigma and promoting awareness of autism. Stigma and misinformation surrounding autism can lead to social isolation and discrimination against individuals with autism. Research can help debunk myths and stereotypes surrounding autism and promote a better understanding of the condition. This can help create a more inclusive society and improve the lives of individuals with autism.

Finally, funding is crucial for supporting autism research. Research is expensive and requires significant resources. Funding from governments, foundations, and private donors is essential for supporting research and developing effective treatments and interventions for autism. Without adequate funding, progress in autism research will be slow, and the development of new treatments and interventions will be limited.

Chapter Eighteen

Emotional Well-being and Autism

Autism, also known as Autism Spectrum Disorder (ASD), is a neurodevelopmental disorder that affects communication, social interaction, and behavior. Although it is typically diagnosed in childhood, individuals with autism continue to experience challenges throughout their lives, including emotional and mental health issues. Below we will explore the emotional well-being of individuals with autism, common challenges they face, and strategies for promoting their emotional health.

One of the biggest challenges for individuals with autism is managing their emotions. They may experience difficulty expressing themselves or understanding the emotions of others, leading to social isolation and frustration. Additionally, individuals with autism may have difficulty regulating their own emotions, resulting in frequent outbursts or meltdowns. This can be especially challenging in social situations or in settings where there are sensory stimuli that can be overwhelming for them.

Another challenge is co-occurring conditions, such as anxiety and depression, which are common among individuals with autism. These conditions can exacerbate the social and communication difficulties associated with autism and lead to feelings of isolation, low self-esteem, and reduced quality of life. Individuals with autism may also experience heightened levels of stress and anxiety due to the challenges they face in navigating the world around them.

It is crucial for individuals with autism to have access to mental health services and support to address these challenges. This can include therapy, medication, and support groups, which can help them develop coping mechanisms and improve their emotional well-being. Additionally, incorporating positive lifestyle habits such as exercise, healthy eating, and relaxation techniques can have a positive impact on emotional health.

Research has shown that mindfulness practices, such as meditation and yoga, can be especially effective in reducing stress and anxiety among individuals with autism. These practices can help them learn to regulate their emotions and develop a greater sense of awareness of their bodies and surroundings. Other therapies, such as cognitive-behavioral therapy and social skills training, can also be effective in helping individuals with autism develop coping mechanisms and improve their emotional well-being.

Another important aspect of emotional well-being for individuals with autism is social support. Having a supportive network of family, friends, and caregivers can make a significant difference in their overall emotional health. Social support can provide a sense of belonging and reduce feelings of isolation, which are common among individuals with autism.

It is also important for society to increase awareness and understanding of autism to promote acceptance and reduce stigma. Individuals with autism face many challenges in their daily lives, and it is important for society to recognize and appreciate their unique strengths and abilities. By promoting a culture of acceptance and understanding, individuals with autism can feel more confident and secure in themselves, which can have a positive impact on their emotional well-being.

Identifying and Managing Emotions

Autism spectrum disorder (ASD) is a developmental disorder that affects an individual's communication, social interaction, and behavior. One of the challenges faced by individuals with ASD is identifying and managing their emotions. Emotional regulation is critical for overall well-being and can have a significant impact on an individual's quality of life. Below we will discuss the challenges that individuals with ASD face in identifying and managing emotions and strategies that can be used to overcome these challenges.

Individuals with ASD often have difficulty understanding their emotions and those of others. They may have trouble interpreting facial expressions, body language, and tone of voice, which makes it difficult for them to understand how others are feeling. This can lead to social isolation and difficulty making friends. It can also lead to difficulty in expressing their own emotions, which can cause frustration and stress.

One of the strategies that can be used to help individuals with ASD identify and manage their emotions is to teach them about emotional vocabulary. This involves teaching them the names of different emotions and how to identify them. This can be done using picture books or other visual aids that show different emotions and the situations that may cause them. Once individuals with ASD can recognize their emotions, they can begin to understand how to manage them.

Another strategy is to use social stories. Social stories are short stories that are designed to help individuals with ASD understand social situations and expectations. They can be used to help individuals understand how to handle emotions in different situations. For example, a social story may describe a situation where a child is feeling angry and how they can calm down.

Another strategy is to use sensory tools to help individuals with ASD manage their emotions. Sensory tools can include things like stress balls, weighted blankets, or fidget toys. These tools can help individuals with ASD feel more grounded and calm, which can help them manage their emotions.

Mindfulness practices can also be beneficial for individuals with ASD. Mindfulness involves being present in the moment and focusing on the present rather than worrying about the future or dwelling on the past. It can help individuals with ASD feel more calm and centered, which can help them manage their emotions.

Exercise is another strategy that can be used to help individuals with ASD manage their emotions. Exercise has been shown to reduce stress and anxiety, and can help individuals feel more relaxed and centered. Exercise can also help individuals with ASD improve their overall health and well-being.

It is important to note that individuals with ASD may require different strategies for identifying and managing their emotions. What works for one individual may not work for another, and it is important to tailor interventions to the individual's specific needs. Additionally, it is important to involve family members and caregivers in the process of identifying and managing emotions. Caregivers can play an important role in helping individuals with ASD recognize their emotions and develop strategies for managing them.

Supporting Mental Health in Individuals with Autism

Supporting Mental Health in Individuals with Autism

Autism Spectrum Disorder (ASD) is a developmental disorder characterized by difficulties in social communication and interaction, restricted and repetitive behaviors and interests, and sensory sensitivities. Autism can also co-occur with a variety of mental health conditions such as anxiety, depression, and attention-deficit/hyperactivity disorder (ADHD). Supporting mental health is a critical aspect of care for individuals with autism, as it can improve overall quality of life and reduce negative outcomes such as suicide and self-harm. Below we will discuss strategies for supporting mental health in individuals with autism.

One essential strategy for supporting mental health in individuals with autism is early identification and intervention for co-occurring conditions. Research has shown that early diagnosis and intervention for mental health conditions can lead to better outcomes and improved quality of life. Therefore, it is essential for clinicians to screen individuals with autism for co-occurring mental health conditions and provide appropriate treatment and support.

Another critical strategy for supporting mental health in individuals with autism is addressing sensory sensitivities. Individuals with autism may have heightened or decreased sensitivity to sensory input, which can be overwhelming and lead to anxiety or distress. It is essential to identify an individual's specific sensory sensitivities and provide accommodations such as noise-cancelling headphones, weighted blankets, or sensory-friendly spaces to reduce sensory overload.

Social skills training is another strategy that can help support mental health in individuals with autism. Social skills training can help individuals with autism learn how to interact with others more effectively, reduce social anxiety, and increase self-esteem. Group therapy, role-playing, and social skills programs can be effective methods for improving social skills in individuals with autism.

Cognitive-behavioral therapy (CBT) is a type of talk therapy that has been shown to be effective in reducing anxiety and depression in individuals with autism. CBT can help individuals learn how to manage their emotions, identify negative thought patterns, and develop coping skills. It is important to find a therapist who is trained in working with individuals with autism and can modify their approach to meet the individual's needs.

Exercise and physical activity can also be effective in improving mental health in individuals with autism. Exercise has been shown to reduce anxiety and depression and improve self-esteem. Individuals with autism may benefit from participating in physical activities that match their interests, such as swimming, hiking, or dancing.

Lastly, it is important to involve the individual with autism in their own care and decision-making. Individuals with autism may have specific preferences or needs that should be taken into consideration when developing a treatment plan. Involving the individual in their care can help improve their sense of control and autonomy, which can lead to improved mental health outcomes.

Building Resilience and Coping Skills

Building Resilience and Coping Skills for Individuals with Autism

Autism, a neurodevelopmental disorder, is known for impairing social communication and interactions, as well as restricted and repetitive behaviors and interests. These symptoms can lead to challenges in everyday life and may impact mental health and overall well-being. While there is no known cure for autism, research has shown that building resilience and coping skills can lead to improved outcomes for individuals with autism. Below we will explore what resilience and coping skills are and how they can be developed to help individuals with autism thrive.

What is resilience?

Resilience can be defined as the ability to adapt and cope with stress and adversity. Resilient individuals are better able to bounce back from setbacks and are able to handle difficult situations with greater ease. Building resilience is important for individuals with autism, who may face unique challenges related to social interactions, communication, and sensory issues.

Resilience is not a trait that individuals are born with, but rather a skill that can be developed and strengthened over time. Research has shown that resilience is influenced by factors such as genetics, early life experiences, and environmental factors. However, individuals can also learn specific skills and strategies to build resilience.

What are coping skills?

Coping skills are strategies that individuals use to manage stress and difficult situations. Coping skills can be both healthy and unhealthy, and it is important to develop healthy coping skills to promote overall well-being.

There are various types of coping skills, including problem-focused coping and emotion-focused coping. Problem-focused coping involves actively addressing the stressor and taking action to solve the problem. Emotion-focused coping involves managing the emotions and feelings associated with the stressor.

Individuals with autism may face unique challenges when it comes to coping with stress and difficult situations. They may struggle with identifying their emotions or communicating their needs to others. Therefore, it is important to develop coping skills that are tailored to their individual needs and abilities.

Building resilience and coping skills for individuals with autism

There are various strategies that can be used to build resilience and coping skills for individuals with autism. Some of these strategies include:

1. Social skills training: Individuals with autism may struggle with social interactions, which can impact their ability to build relationships and cope with stress. Social skills training can help individuals learn how to communicate effectively, read social cues, and manage social situations.

2. Cognitive-behavioral therapy: Cognitive-behavioral therapy (CBT) is a type of therapy that helps individuals identify and change negative thought patterns and behaviors. CBT can be tailored to address specific challenges related to autism, such as anxiety, sensory issues, and social communication.

3. Mindfulness practices: Mindfulness practices, such as meditation and yoga, can help individuals with autism manage stress and improve emotional regulation. Mindfulness practices can also help individuals become more aware of their thoughts and emotions, which can lead to improved self-awareness and coping skills.

4. Sensory integration therapy: Sensory integration therapy involves activities that are designed to help individuals with autism regulate their sensory input. This can include activities such as swinging, bouncing, and playing with textured materials. Sensory integration therapy can help individuals with autism manage sensory issues and reduce stress and anxiety.

5. Physical activity: Regular physical activity has been shown to have numerous benefits for individuals with autism, including improved mood, increased social interaction, and improved cognitive functioning. Physical activity can also provide an outlet for individuals to manage stress and improve overall well-being.

Chapter Nineteen

Autism and Spirituality

Autism is a neurodevelopmental disorder that affects social communication and interaction. It is a complex condition that can have various impacts on an individual's life, including their spiritual development. Spirituality is a broad concept that can encompass religion, faith, belief, and a sense of connection to a higher power or purpose. It can play an important role in providing a sense of meaning and purpose in life, and for some individuals with autism, it can provide a source of comfort and support.

However, due to the social communication difficulties that come with autism, many individuals may struggle with understanding and connecting with traditional religious practices and beliefs. This can lead to feelings of isolation and exclusion, which can have a negative impact on mental health and well-being.

It is important for individuals with autism to have the opportunity to explore their spirituality in a way that is meaningful to them. This may involve finding alternative ways to connect with their faith or beliefs, such as through art, music, nature, or other forms of expression. It may also involve finding a supportive community that understands and accepts their unique needs and challenges.

There are also programs and resources available to help individuals with autism explore their spirituality and develop coping skills. For example, some religious organizations offer adapted services and accommodations for individuals with disabilities, such as sensory-friendly spaces or sign language interpretation. There are also support groups and therapy programs that incorporate spirituality and mindfulness practices to help individuals with autism manage stress and anxiety.

It is important to note that spirituality is a personal and individual experience, and what works for one person may not work for another. Therefore, it is essential to provide individuals with autism with a range of options and opportunities to explore their spirituality in a way that is meaningful and relevant to them.

Another important consideration is the role of spirituality in the lives of families and caregivers of individuals with autism. Caring for a loved one with autism can be challenging and stressful, and spirituality can provide a source of strength and support during difficult times. It is important to recognize the unique needs and experiences of families and caregivers and provide them with resources and support to help them maintain their own well-being.

Exploring Spirituality and Faith in the Context of Autism

Autism is a complex neurodevelopmental disorder that affects an individual's social interaction, communication, and behavior. Autism is often associated with difficulties in social interactions, which can make it difficult for individuals to connect with others, form relationships, and engage in spiritual practices. However, research has shown that individuals with autism can and do engage in spirituality and faith in meaningful ways. Below we will explore the relationship between autism and spirituality and how individuals with autism can benefit from engaging in spiritual practices.

Spirituality can be defined as the search for a sense of meaning and purpose in life. It is often linked to religion, but it is not the same thing. Spirituality can be a personal and subjective experience, and it can be experienced in many different ways. Faith, on the other hand, refers to a belief in a particular religion or set of religious beliefs. Many people find that spirituality and faith are closely linked and that engaging in spiritual practices can help them feel more connected to a higher power, to others, and to the world around them.

Individuals with autism may struggle with social interactions, communication, and sensory issues, which can make it difficult for them to engage in spiritual practices. For example, attending religious services may be overwhelming for someone with sensory issues, and social interactions in those settings can be difficult. However, research has shown that individuals with autism can benefit from engaging in spiritual practices, and that faith communities can be a valuable source of support for individuals with autism and their families.

One of the benefits of engaging in spiritual practices is that they can provide a sense of structure and routine, which can be especially helpful for individuals with autism. Spiritual practices can help individuals with autism feel a sense of purpose and belonging, which can help them feel more connected to their community. Engaging in spiritual practices can also help individuals with autism develop coping strategies for dealing with stress and anxiety.

Faith communities can be a valuable source of support for individuals with autism and their families. Some religious organizations have established support groups specifically for families of children with autism. These groups can provide a safe space for families to share their experiences and learn from one another. Faith communities can also provide practical support for families, such as respite care, transportation to appointments, and assistance with finding resources in the community.

Research has shown that spirituality and faith can have positive effects on mental health and well-being. For example, engaging in spiritual practices has been linked to lower levels of anxiety and depression. It has also been shown to increase resilience and coping skills, which can be especially important for individuals with autism who may face additional challenges in their daily lives.

It is important to note that spirituality and faith are not a substitute for professional medical or psychological treatment. While engaging in spiritual practices can be helpful for individuals with autism, it is important to seek out professional treatment when necessary. Additionally, it is important to ensure that individuals with autism are not excluded or stigmatized within faith communities.

Inclusivity and Support in Religious Communities

Inclusivity and support in religious communities are important for individuals with autism. It is essential to create an environment that is welcoming and accommodating for people of all abilities. Unfortunately, many religious institutions may not have the knowledge or resources to provide adequate support for those with autism.

Autism is a neurological condition that affects communication, social interaction, and behavior. People with autism may experience sensory overload, have difficulty processing social cues, and struggle with changes in routine. These challenges can make it difficult for them to feel comfortable in traditional religious settings.

Fortunately, many religious organizations are beginning to recognize the importance of inclusivity and support for people with autism. Some churches, synagogues, mosques, and temples have created programs specifically for individuals with autism and their families. These programs provide a safe space for worship and social interaction while accommodating the unique needs of those with autism.

One example of this is the Autism Inclusion Program (AIP) at Temple Beth-El in Birmingham, Alabama. This program provides support and accommodations for individuals with autism during religious services and events. The AIP includes trained volunteers who provide one-on-one support and assistance, sensory-friendly rooms, and visual schedules to help individuals with autism feel comfortable and included in religious activities.

Similarly, the Autism and Faith Program at the University of Tennessee in Knoxville provides training and resources to religious leaders to create more inclusive and supportive environments for people with autism. This program offers guidance on adapting religious practices to accommodate sensory sensitivities and communication difficulties, as well as information on how to support families affected by autism.

Creating inclusive environments for people with autism also involves educating the community on the challenges and strengths of autism. Religious leaders and members can learn about autism and how to support individuals with autism through training programs and workshops.

In addition, there are many resources available to religious communities looking to create more inclusive environments for individuals with autism. The Autism Society, for example, provides resources and training on autism awareness and inclusion, including a Faith-Based Initiative that offers guidance and support to religious organizations.

Inclusivity and support in religious communities not only benefit individuals with autism but also enrich the entire community. By creating a welcoming and accommodating environment, religious organizations can provide opportunities for individuals with autism to connect with others and engage in meaningful activities.

Moreover, promoting inclusivity and support in religious communities is essential for breaking down barriers and reducing stigma associated with autism. By creating awareness and understanding of autism, religious organizations can help foster acceptance and promote a culture of inclusivity.

The Role of Spiritual Practices in Emotional Well-being

The relationship between spirituality and emotional well-being has been a subject of interest and investigation for centuries. For individuals with autism, who may experience social and emotional challenges, exploring spiritual practices can offer unique opportunities for personal growth and development. Below we will explore the role of spiritual practices in promoting emotional well-being in individuals with autism.

Spirituality can be defined as a sense of connection to something greater than oneself, including a higher power, nature, or the universe. Spiritual practices can involve a range of activities, such as prayer, meditation, yoga, or mindfulness. These practices have been shown to be beneficial for individuals with autism, particularly in promoting emotional regulation and reducing anxiety.

One study conducted by the University of Missouri found that mindfulness-based interventions were effective in reducing anxiety and promoting emotional regulation in individuals with autism. The study used a combination of mindfulness practices, including breath awareness, body scan, and walking meditation, to promote awareness of thoughts, feelings, and bodily sensations. The study found that after six weeks of practice, participants experienced significant reductions in anxiety and improvements in emotional regulation.

Prayer and meditation have also been shown to be beneficial for individuals with autism. A study published in the Journal of Autism and Developmental Disorders found that prayer and meditation were effective in reducing stress and anxiety in parents of children with autism. The study found that prayer and meditation were particularly helpful in promoting a sense of calmness and perspective, as well as reducing feelings of guilt and self-blame.

Yoga is another spiritual practice that has been shown to be effective in promoting emotional well-being in individuals with autism. A study published in the Journal of Alternative and Complementary Medicine found that a six-month yoga program was effective in reducing anxiety and improving social functioning in children with autism. The program involved a combination of yoga postures, breathing exercises, and relaxation techniques.

In addition to promoting emotional regulation and reducing anxiety, spiritual practices can also offer individuals with autism a sense of purpose and meaning. For some individuals, this may involve exploring religious traditions and practices. For others, spirituality may involve a connection to nature or the universe.

However, it is important to note that not all individuals with autism may be interested in exploring spiritual practices, and it is important to respect each individual's beliefs and preferences. Additionally, it is important to consider cultural and religious differences and the potential for cultural bias when implementing spiritual practices.

Chapter Twenty

Autism and Gender

Autism spectrum disorder (ASD) affects individuals across all genders, races, and ethnicities. However, research has shown that there are significant differences in the prevalence and diagnosis of ASD between genders. Below we will explore the complexities of autism and gender, including the current research, diagnostic challenges, and potential implications for treatment and support.

According to the Centers for Disease Control and Prevention (CDC), autism is about 4.3 times more common in boys than in girls. This gender disparity has led to a general assumption that autism is a "male" disorder. However, recent studies suggest that this assumption may be flawed. In fact, some researchers argue that the gender gap in autism may be largely a result of biases in the diagnostic process.

For example, girls with autism may exhibit different symptoms than boys and may be better at masking their symptoms in social situations. This means that girls may be more likely to go undiagnosed or misdiagnosed with other conditions. Additionally, diagnostic criteria for autism have historically been based on research with male participants, which may not fully capture the experiences of girls and women with autism.

Research suggests that girls with autism may be more likely to have co-occurring mental health conditions, such as anxiety and depression, than boys with autism. They may also have more difficulty with social communication and may be more likely to have restricted interests that are considered "typical" for girls, such as a fascination with animals or dolls. These differences may contribute to the under-diagnosis or misdiagnosis of girls with autism.

The under-diagnosis of girls with autism has significant implications for treatment and support. If girls are not properly diagnosed with autism, they may not receive appropriate interventions and accommodations that can help them succeed in school, work, and social relationships. They may also be at risk for developing mental health conditions, such as anxiety and depression, which can further impact their well-being.

There is a growing need for research on the experiences of girls and women with autism. This research should focus on identifying the unique characteristics and symptoms of autism in girls and women, as well as exploring the ways in which gender identity and expression intersect with autism. By better understanding the complexities of autism and gender, we can improve the diagnostic process and provide more targeted interventions and support for individuals across the gender spectrum.

Another important aspect of autism and gender is the experiences of transgender and non-binary individuals. Limited research has been conducted on the prevalence and experiences of autism among these individuals. However, some studies suggest that transgender and non-binary individuals may be more likely to be diagnosed with autism than cisgender individuals.

This may be because individuals who are transgender or non-binary may experience higher levels of social stigma and discrimination, which can lead to increased stress and anxiety. Additionally, they may have different experiences with social communication and may be more likely to have restricted interests that are considered atypical for their gender identity.

However, more research is needed to fully understand the relationship between autism and gender identity.

The Presentation of Autism in Girls and Women

Autism is a neurodevelopmental disorder that affects individuals across the gender spectrum. However, historically, autism has been associated with males, and this has led to underdiagnosis and misdiagnosis in females. Research indicates that autism is more prevalent in males, but this does not mean that females do not have autism. Below we will discuss the presentation of autism in girls and women, the reasons for underdiagnosis, and the challenges females with autism face.

1. Autism is a complex disorder that affects an individual's communication, social interaction, and behavior. Research indicates that autism affects males more than females, with a ratio of 4:1. However, the actual prevalence of autism in females may be higher than previously thought due to underdiagnosis and misdiagnosis. One reason for this is that the diagnostic criteria for autism have been based primarily on research conducted on males. The criteria focus on the more stereotypical presentation of autism, which may not be as evident in females with autism.

Females with autism may have different symptoms than males, and these may be more subtle. For example, girls with autism may be more social than boys, but their social interactions may be superficial and lack emotional depth. Girls may also develop coping mechanisms that allow them to camouflage their autistic traits, such as imitating their peers' behavior or memorizing social scripts. This can make it challenging for clinicians to recognize the signs of autism in girls and diagnose them accurately.

Furthermore, the symptoms of autism in girls may present differently from those in boys. For instance, females with autism may have more difficulties with social communication and emotional regulation than with repetitive behaviors and restricted interests. They may also struggle with nonverbal communication, such as making eye contact, interpreting facial expressions, and using gestures appropriately. These symptoms may be less evident in girls, making it more challenging to diagnose autism.

Another reason for underdiagnosis and misdiagnosis is the stigma associated with autism. Girls with autism may face additional challenges, such as negative stereotypes and misconceptions about their gender. The idea that girls are supposed to be social and empathetic may lead to the assumption that girls cannot have autism. This can prevent girls from being diagnosed, as clinicians may not consider autism as a possibility.

Females with autism may also experience challenges related to mental health. They may be at a higher risk of developing anxiety, depression, and other mental health conditions due to the social and emotional difficulties they face. These challenges may be further compounded by the lack of understanding and awareness of autism in girls and women.

The challenges that girls and women with autism face highlight the need for a more inclusive and gender-sensitive approach to autism diagnosis and treatment. Clinicians need to be aware of the different ways in which autism can present in females and should use gender-sensitive diagnostic criteria that take into account the unique needs and experiences of girls and women with autism. This requires a shift in the way autism is perceived and understood, from a predominantly male-oriented perspective to a more inclusive and gender-sensitive approach.

Addressing Gender Bias in Autism Diagnosis and Treatment

Autism is a neurodevelopmental disorder that affects individuals in different ways. Historically, autism has been diagnosed more frequently in males than females. This has led to significant gender bias in the diagnosis and treatment of autism. Research suggests that girls and women with autism may present differently than boys and men, and they may be underdiagnosed or misdiagnosed.

One of the reasons for the underdiagnosis of autism in females is that autism diagnostic tools were developed primarily using male subjects. Autism is often characterized by repetitive behaviors, restricted interests, and difficulty with social interaction and communication. These symptoms may be more obvious in males than in females. Girls and women with autism may have developed strategies to mask their difficulties in social situations, making it more difficult for clinicians to recognize their symptoms.

Research has shown that females with autism may present with different symptoms than males. Girls with autism tend to have better social skills than boys, and they may be more socially motivated. They may also have different interests and play styles than their male counterparts. In addition, females with autism may be more likely to have comorbidities such as anxiety or depression, which can further complicate diagnosis and treatment.

Another issue in the diagnosis of autism in females is the misconception that autism is a male disorder. This stereotype is perpetuated by media portrayals of autism and the lack of representation of females with autism in research studies. This bias can prevent clinicians from considering autism as a diagnosis in females, even when they present with symptoms.

The underdiagnosis and misdiagnosis of females with autism can have significant consequences. Delayed diagnosis can lead to a lack of access to appropriate support and interventions. Females with autism may be more likely to develop mental health issues such as anxiety and depression, and they may struggle with academic and social development. Additionally, the lack of diagnosis can lead to feelings of isolation and confusion, as females with autism may not understand why they are different from their peers.

To address the issue of gender bias in autism diagnosis and treatment, it is important to increase awareness and education among clinicians and the general public. Clinicians should be trained to recognize the different ways that autism may present in females and to consider autism as a diagnosis in all individuals, regardless of gender. There should also be more research focused on the presentation of autism in females and the development of diagnostic tools that are sensitive to gender differences.

In addition, there is a need for greater representation of females with autism in media and research studies. This will help to break down stereotypes and increase awareness of the diversity of individuals with autism. By promoting a more inclusive and accurate understanding of autism, we can better support individuals of all genders who are living with the disorder.

Finally, it is important to recognize that autism is a spectrum disorder, and individuals with autism may have different needs and experiences. It is crucial to provide individualized support and interventions that meet the unique needs of each person. By providing appropriate support and accommodations, individuals with autism can lead fulfilling and meaningful lives.

Supporting Transgender and Nonbinary Individuals with Autism

Supporting Transgender and Nonbinary Individuals with Autism

Autism is a neurological condition that affects the way a person perceives and interacts with the world. Individuals with autism often experience difficulties with social communication and interaction, as well as sensory processing and repetitive behaviors. However, there is significant diversity within the autism community, including individuals who identify as transgender or nonbinary. These individuals face unique challenges related to their gender identity and their autism diagnosis, and it is important to understand and address these challenges in order to provide effective support.

The term transgender refers to individuals whose gender identity does not match the sex they were assigned at birth. Nonbinary individuals identify as neither entirely male nor entirely female, or they may feel that their gender identity is not accurately described by the binary categories of male and female. Research suggests that the prevalence of gender dysphoria, or distress related to one's gender identity, is higher among individuals with autism than in the general population. This may be due in part to the fact that people with autism often experience social difficulties and struggle to conform to societal expectations of gender roles and behavior.

One of the most significant challenges facing transgender and nonbinary individuals with autism is the difficulty of obtaining a diagnosis and appropriate treatment. Many healthcare providers are not trained to recognize the unique experiences of transgender and nonbinary individuals, and may not understand the potential intersection of autism and gender identity. This can lead to misdiagnosis or a lack of diagnosis altogether, which can have serious negative consequences for the individual's mental health and well-being.

Even when a diagnosis is obtained, there may be limited resources available for transgender and nonbinary individuals with autism. Many gender clinics and support groups may not have the specific expertise needed to address the complex needs of this population. Additionally, many interventions for autism may be designed with binary gender categories in mind, which may not be relevant or appropriate for transgender and nonbinary individuals.

In order to provide effective support for transgender and nonbinary individuals with autism, it is important to take a holistic approach that addresses both their autism diagnosis and their gender identity. This may involve working with healthcare providers who are knowledgeable about both autism and gender identity, as well as seeking out resources and support groups that are specifically designed for transgender and nonbinary individuals with autism.

One potential intervention that may be helpful for this population is social skills training that addresses gender identity and expression. This may include activities that promote self-expression and assertiveness, as well as strategies for navigating social situations in a way that feels authentic and comfortable for the individual.

It is also important to address the unique challenges that transgender and nonbinary individuals with autism may face in terms of sensory processing and executive function. For example, some individuals may experience sensory sensitivities related to certain gendered clothing or hairstyles, or may struggle to understand social cues related to gender expression. It may be helpful to provide sensory accommodations, such as clothing made from comfortable materials or noise-cancelling headphones, as well as targeted instruction on social skills related to gender identity.

Finally, it is crucial to create a supportive and inclusive environment for transgender and nonbinary individuals with autism. This includes recognizing and respecting their preferred pronouns and names, as well as creating spaces where they feel safe and accepted. It may also involve challenging gender stereotypes and norms within the autism community, and working to create a more diverse and inclusive understanding of what it means to be autistic.

Chapter Twenty-One

Travel and Leisure with Autism

Travel and Leisure with Autism

Autism is a neurodevelopmental disorder that affects an individual's ability to communicate, socialize, and interact with others. It can also impact a person's sensory processing, making it difficult to process stimuli such as sounds, sights, smells, and textures. Travel and leisure activities can be a challenge for individuals with autism due to changes in routine, unfamiliar environments, and sensory overload. However, with the right preparation and support, travel and leisure can be enjoyable and enriching experiences for individuals with autism and their families.

Preparing for Travel

Preparing for travel is crucial for individuals with autism. Familiarizing oneself with the destination and planning for any potential sensory triggers can help alleviate anxiety and make the experience more enjoyable. Researching the destination ahead of time, including the culture, customs, and laws, can help prevent any unexpected surprises that could be overwhelming for individuals with autism.

Additionally, preparing for the actual journey itself is important. Individuals with autism may have difficulty with unexpected changes or disruptions in routine, so it is essential to plan ahead and communicate any potential changes. For example, individuals with autism may struggle with airport security, so notifying the TSA in advance and requesting accommodations such as a private screening can help ease anxiety and make the experience less stressful.

Accommodations and Support

When traveling, accommodations and support can make a significant difference for individuals with autism. Many airports and airlines offer services such as pre-boarding and early check-in for individuals with disabilities, which can help reduce stress and sensory overload. Some airlines also offer sensory-friendly flights that are designed to reduce noise and lights, creating a calmer environment for individuals with autism.

Hotels and resorts can also provide accommodations such as sensory rooms, quiet hours, and special menus for individuals with dietary restrictions or sensory processing issues. It is essential to communicate any needs or concerns with the hotel staff in advance to ensure a comfortable and enjoyable stay.

Leisure Activities

Participating in leisure activities can be a fun and enriching experience for individuals with autism. However, it is important to consider the individual's sensory processing and communication abilities when selecting activities. Activities that are overstimulating or require complex communication may be overwhelming for individuals with autism, so it is crucial to find activities that are enjoyable and manageable for the individual.

Many tourist attractions, such as museums and theme parks, offer accommodations such as quiet rooms and sensory-friendly events. Additionally, outdoor activities such as hiking and nature walks can be a calming and enjoyable experience for individuals with autism. It is important to plan ahead and research potential activities to ensure they are a good fit for the individual's needs and abilities.

Planning and Preparing for Travel with Autism

Travelling with autism can be challenging, but it can also be a rewarding and enjoyable experience with the proper planning and preparation. Autism is a neurodevelopmental disorder that affects communication, social interaction, and behavior. These challenges can make travelling stressful and overwhelming for individuals with autism and their families. However, with some preparation and knowledge, individuals with autism can have positive travel experiences.

Planning ahead is essential for a successful trip. This can include selecting a destination that is suitable for the individual's needs, researching accommodations and transportation options, and creating a detailed itinerary. When choosing a destination, consider the individual's sensory needs and interests. Some destinations may be too loud, crowded, or overwhelming for individuals with autism. It is important to research the local customs and culture to ensure that the individual's needs are met.

When selecting accommodations, consider the individual's sensory needs and preferences. Many hotels and resorts offer sensory-friendly rooms with calming colors, minimal décor, and special lighting. Some accommodations may also provide noise-cancelling headphones, weighted blankets, or other sensory tools to help individuals with autism feel comfortable.

Transportation can also be a challenge for individuals with autism. Consider the individual's comfort level with different modes of transportation, such as airplanes, trains, or buses. Many airlines offer special assistance for individuals with disabilities, including pre-boarding, seating accommodations, and wheelchair assistance. It is important to contact the airline ahead of time to discuss the individual's needs and make necessary arrangements.

Creating a detailed itinerary can also help reduce stress and anxiety for individuals with autism. Plan out each day's activities, including rest periods and sensory breaks. This can help the individual feel more in control of the trip and reduce the likelihood of meltdowns or sensory overload.

In addition to planning ahead, it is important to prepare the individual with autism for the trip. This can include using visual schedules, social stories, or other communication tools to help the individual understand what to expect on the trip. Practicing unfamiliar routines, such as going through airport security or boarding a plane, can also help the individual feel more comfortable with the process.

Travelling with autism can also be an opportunity for growth and learning. Exposing individuals with autism to new experiences and cultures can help broaden their horizons and build new skills. For example, visiting a new city or country can provide opportunities to practice social skills, learn new languages, and develop problem-solving skills.

It is also important to consider the individual's interests and hobbies when planning travel. Many individuals with autism have special interests that can be incorporated into the trip, such as visiting museums, zoos, or other attractions. These activities can be used to help the individual feel more engaged and motivated throughout the trip.

Tips for Making Travel Accessible and Enjoyable

Traveling can be a fun and exciting experience for many people, but for individuals with autism, it can also be a challenging one. Changes in routine, sensory overload, and unfamiliar environments can cause stress and anxiety, making it difficult for individuals with autism and their families to enjoy travel. However, with careful planning and preparation, travel can be made accessible and enjoyable for individuals with autism. Below we will discuss some tips for making travel accessible and enjoyable for individuals with autism.

The first tip is to plan ahead. It's important to research your destination and accommodations in advance to ensure they are suitable for individuals with autism. Consider the layout of the hotel or rental property, proximity to attractions, and noise level. It's also a good idea to inquire about any available sensory-friendly accommodations, such as dimmed lighting, noise-cancelling headphones, and weighted blankets. Many hotels and rental properties offer these amenities, but it's important to inquire in advance to ensure they are available.

The second tip is to create a visual schedule. Individuals with autism often benefit from a visual schedule, which can help them understand and prepare for what's to come. Before the trip, create a visual schedule with pictures or symbols that represent each activity or destination on the itinerary. This can help individuals with autism understand the sequence of events and reduce anxiety.

The third tip is to pack familiar items. Bringing familiar items from home, such as a favorite toy, blanket, or stuffed animal, can provide comfort and reduce anxiety for individuals with autism. Familiar items can also help them transition to unfamiliar environments more easily.

The fourth tip is to consider transportation. Traveling by car or train may be more comfortable and less overwhelming than flying for some individuals with autism. If flying is necessary, it's important to prepare for the sensory overload that can come with air travel. Noise-cancelling headphones and a weighted blanket can help reduce sensory input, and TSA Cares is a program that provides assistance for individuals with disabilities going through airport security.

The fifth tip is to bring sensory tools. Sensory tools such as fidget toys, chew toys, and sensory balls can help individuals with autism regulate their sensory input and reduce anxiety. It's important to pack these tools in a carry-on bag or easily accessible location for easy access during travel.

The sixth tip is to communicate with travel partners. Communication is key when traveling with individuals with autism. It's important to communicate with travel partners, including family members and travel guides, about the individual's needs and preferences. This can include communication methods, dietary restrictions, and sensory needs.

The seventh tip is to take breaks. Traveling can be overwhelming, so it's important to take breaks throughout the day to rest and recharge. Schedule breaks into the itinerary and plan activities that are calming and relaxing, such as a nature walk or yoga session.

The eighth tip is to be flexible. It's important to be flexible when traveling with individuals with autism, as unexpected changes in routine or environment can cause stress and anxiety. Be prepared to make adjustments to the itinerary as needed and allow for breaks when necessary.

Autism-Friendly Destinations and Attractions

Autism is a neurodevelopmental disorder that affects a person's ability to communicate, socialize, and understand the world around them. Traveling can be a challenging experience for individuals with autism due to the sensory overload and changes in routine that can occur during the journey. However, with some planning and preparation, it is possible to make travel more accessible and enjoyable for people with autism. Below we will explore some tips and destinations that are autism-friendly.

When planning a trip with someone who has autism, it is essential to consider their specific needs and preferences. For example, some individuals may have sensory sensitivities to certain sounds or textures, while others may require a structured routine. To prepare for the trip, it may be helpful to create a visual schedule of the journey, including any transitions, such as check-in, security, and boarding. This schedule can help reduce anxiety and provide a sense of predictability.

Another useful tip is to inform the airline or other transportation providers about any special needs before the trip. This can include requesting early boarding, a seat near the bathroom, or special meals. Some airlines may also provide noise-cancelling headphones or sensory toys to help individuals with autism feel more comfortable during the flight.

Choosing an autism-friendly destination is also crucial. Some cities and attractions have taken steps to make their environments more accessible and inclusive for people with autism. For example, Sesame Place in Pennsylvania is the world's first autism-certified theme park, with trained staff and quiet areas for sensory breaks. Legoland parks in Florida and California have also implemented similar measures, such as designated quiet rooms and lowered sound levels on certain attractions.

In addition to theme parks, there are also many other autism-friendly destinations to consider. National parks and nature reserves can provide a calming and stimulating environment for individuals with autism. For example, Yellowstone National Park offers ranger-led programs for children with autism, as well as sensory backpacks that include noise-cancelling headphones, fidget toys, and visual aids. Disney Cruise Line also offers autism-friendly experiences, such as a "quiet room" and specially trained counselors for children with autism.

It is also essential to consider accommodations when traveling with someone with autism. Many hotels and resorts offer special accommodations, such as sensory-friendly rooms and quiet floors. For example, the Marriott hotels in the UK and Ireland have launched a "Autism Friendly Rooms" initiative that includes low lighting, sensory toys, and a separate lounge area for families. Some hotels also offer special rates or discounts for families with autism.

Finally, it is important to remember that every person with autism is unique and may have different needs and preferences. It is essential to communicate with the individual and their family or caregivers to understand what accommodations and support they may require. With some planning and preparation, travel can be a fun and enriching experience for individuals with autism.

Chapter Twenty-Two

Autism and the Law

Autism is a developmental disorder that can impact an individual's ability to communicate, socialize, and interact with others. In recent years, there has been increasing awareness and understanding of autism, leading to changes in laws and policies that affect individuals on the autism spectrum. However, there are still many areas where individuals with autism face challenges and barriers, and where the law can play a role in addressing these issues.

One area where the law is particularly relevant for individuals with autism is in the realm of education. The Individuals with Disabilities Education Act (IDEA) is a federal law that requires public schools to provide special education services to students with disabilities, including autism. This can include individualized education plans (IEPs) that outline specific goals and accommodations for the student, as well as services such as speech therapy, occupational therapy, and social skills training. IDEA is an important tool for ensuring that students with autism receive the support they need to succeed in school.

Another important legal issue for individuals with autism is employment. The Americans with Disabilities Act (ADA) prohibits discrimination against individuals with disabilities in employment, including individuals with autism. This means that employers cannot discriminate against someone with autism in hiring, firing, or other employment decisions. Employers are also required to provide reasonable accommodations to employees with disabilities, including individuals with autism, to ensure that they can perform their job duties effectively. For example, an employee with autism might need a quiet workspace or additional time to complete tasks.

In addition to IDEA and the ADA, there are other laws and policies that can impact individuals with autism. For example, the Affordable Care Act (ACA) includes provisions that require insurance companies to cover behavioral health treatments for children with autism, such as applied behavior analysis (ABA) therapy. This has made these treatments more accessible and affordable for families of children with autism.

However, there are still many areas where individuals with autism face challenges and where the law can play a role in addressing these issues. For example, many individuals with autism struggle with navigating the legal system, particularly when it comes to issues such as guardianship, housing, and benefits. There is a need for more resources and support for individuals with autism and their families in navigating these systems and accessing the support they need.

Another area of concern is the criminal justice system. Individuals with autism may be at increased risk of being involved in the criminal justice system due to difficulties with social communication and interaction, as well as sensory processing issues that can make certain situations overwhelming. There is a need for training and education for law enforcement officers and others in the criminal justice system to better understand autism and how to effectively interact with individuals on the spectrum.

Finally, there is a need for more research and advocacy around the issue of autism and the law. This includes research on the experiences of individuals with autism in the legal system, as well as advocacy efforts to ensure that the legal rights and needs of individuals with autism are being adequately addressed.

Understanding Legal Rights and Protections

Autism is a neurodevelopmental disorder that affects communication, social interaction, and behavior. While individuals with autism have the same legal rights as everyone else, they may require additional support and accommodations to ensure they are not discriminated against in various areas of life. Understanding the legal rights and protections available to individuals with autism is crucial for creating a more inclusive and supportive society.

The Americans with Disabilities Act (ADA) is a federal law that prohibits discrimination against individuals with disabilities in all areas of public life, including employment, education, and access to public facilities and services. The ADA defines a disability as a physical or mental impairment that substantially limits one or more major life activities. This definition includes autism, and individuals with autism are protected under the ADA.

In the workplace, individuals with autism have the right to request reasonable accommodations that will enable them to perform their job duties. Reasonable accommodations may include modifying work schedules, providing additional training or support, or modifying the work environment to reduce sensory distractions. Employers are required by law to provide reasonable accommodations, as long as doing so does not create undue hardship.

In the education system, students with autism are protected by the Individuals with Disabilities Education Act (IDEA). This law mandates that all children with disabilities, including autism, receive a free appropriate public education (FAPE). Schools are required to develop an Individualized Education Program (IEP) for each student with autism, which outlines their educational goals and the support and services they require to meet those goals. These services may include special education classes, speech therapy, occupational therapy, and behavioral interventions.

The IDEA also requires that schools provide students with a least restrictive environment (LRE), meaning that students with disabilities should be educated in the same setting as their peers without disabilities as much as possible. This may mean that a student with autism attends a general education classroom with support from a paraprofessional or special education teacher.

Outside of the workplace and education system, individuals with autism are also protected by laws that ensure their access to public facilities and services. For example, the ADA requires that public buildings and transportation systems be accessible to individuals with disabilities, including those with autism. This may mean providing ramps, elevators, or other accommodations that enable individuals with autism to access these facilities.

In addition to legal protections, advocacy and support organizations play an important role in promoting the rights of individuals with autism. These organizations work to educate the public about autism and the challenges faced by individuals with autism and their families. They also advocate for policies and practices that promote inclusion and accessibility for individuals with autism.

The Autism Society of America is one such organization that provides advocacy and support for individuals with autism and their families. The organization works to promote understanding and acceptance of autism, as well as providing resources and support to individuals with autism and their families.

Another organization, Autism Speaks, is dedicated to promoting research into the causes and treatments of autism, as well as promoting policies and practices that improve the lives of individuals with autism and their families. The organization also provides resources and support to individuals with autism and their families.

Navigating Disability Benefits and Services

Navigating Disability Benefits and Services for Autism

Autism is a developmental disorder that can significantly impact a person's life, particularly in the areas of communication, social interaction, and behavior. For individuals with autism, managing daily life can be challenging, and accessing the appropriate support and services can be essential. Fortunately, there are several disability benefits and services available to help individuals with autism live fulfilling lives. Below we will explore the various disability benefits and services available to people with autism and how to navigate them.

One of the most important things to consider when navigating disability benefits and services is eligibility. The eligibility criteria for different services may vary, and it is crucial to know what requirements must be met to qualify for a particular benefit or service. Typically, the eligibility criteria may include age, income level, and level of disability. Some disability benefits and services available to individuals with autism include:

1. Social Security Disability Benefits: Social Security Disability Benefits (SSDI) are available to individuals who have paid into the Social Security system and have a disability that is severe enough to prevent them

from working. The Social Security Administration (SSA) has a list of impairments that they use to determine eligibility, and autism is one of the conditions on the list. To qualify for SSDI, individuals with autism must meet the eligibility requirements, including having a severe and persistent impairment that impacts their ability to work and earn a living.

2. Supplemental Security Income: Supplemental Security Income (SSI) is a needs-based program that provides financial assistance to individuals with disabilities who have limited income and resources. Unlike SSDI, SSI is not based on work history, and it is available to children and adults with disabilities. To qualify for SSI, individuals with autism must meet the eligibility requirements, including having a severe and persistent impairment that impacts their ability to work and earn a living.

3. Medicaid: Medicaid is a federal and state-funded program that provides health insurance to individuals with low income and resources. Medicaid is available to children and adults with disabilities and can provide coverage for a wide range of medical services, including doctor visits, hospitalizations, medications, and therapies. To qualify for Medicaid, individuals with autism must meet the eligibility requirements, including having a low income and limited resources.

4. Early Intervention Services: Early Intervention Services are designed to help young children with disabilities develop and reach their full potential. Early Intervention Services are available to children from birth to three years old and can include therapies such as speech and language therapy, occupational therapy, and physical therapy. To qualify for Early Intervention Services, children must be evaluated and diagnosed with a developmental delay or disability.

5. Special Education Services: Special Education Services are provided by public schools and are designed to help students with disabilities access

a free and appropriate education. Special Education Services can include individualized education plans (IEPs), classroom accommodations, and specialized instruction. To qualify for Special Education Services, students must be evaluated and diagnosed with a disability.

Navigating disability benefits and services can be challenging, but there are several resources available to help individuals and families. Some useful resources include:

6. The Social Security Administration: The Social Security Administration (SSA) is responsible for administering SSDI and SSI, and they have a website that provides information about disability benefits and services.

7. The Centers for Medicare and Medicaid Services: The Centers for Medicare and Medicaid Services (CMS) is responsible for administering Medicaid, and they have a website that provides information about the program.

8. The National Early Childhood Technical Assistance Center: The National Early Childhood Technical Assistance Center (NECTAC) provides resources and technical assistance to families and professionals who work with young children with disabilities.

9. The National Center for Learning Disabilities: The National Center for Learning Disabilities (NCLD) provides resources and support to individuals with learning disabilities

Advocating for Policy Change and Legislation

Advocating for Policy Change and Legislation

Autism is a complex neurodevelopmental disorder that affects millions of individuals and families worldwide. While significant progress has been made in the understanding and treatment of autism, there is still a long way to go in terms of advocating for policies that support individuals with autism and their families. Below we will discuss the importance of advocating for policy change and legislation in relation to autism, highlighting some of the key issues facing individuals with autism and their families, as well as the role that advocacy can play in driving change.

One of the biggest challenges facing individuals with autism and their families is access to services and support. In many countries, there is a lack of funding for autism services, which can make it difficult for families to access the resources they need to support their loved ones with autism. This can include everything from early intervention programs to specialized therapies and services. Advocacy can play a critical role in pushing for increased funding and resources for autism services, as well as in raising awareness about the need for better access to these services.

Another issue facing individuals with autism and their families is discrimination and stigma. Unfortunately, there is still a significant amount of ignorance and misinformation surrounding autism, which can lead to discrimination and exclusion. This can manifest in a number of ways, from difficulty accessing education and employment opportunities to social isolation and exclusion from community activities. Advocacy can help to challenge these negative stereotypes and promote a more inclusive and accepting society for individuals with autism.

Legislation is another important area of advocacy when it comes to autism. There are a number of legal issues that can impact individuals with autism and their families, from access to healthcare and education to discrimination and employment. Advocacy can help to ensure that there are legal protections in place to support individuals with autism and their families, as well as to promote policies that are inclusive and supportive of individuals with autism.

In addition to advocating for policy change and legislation, there are a number of other ways that individuals and organizations can support individuals with autism and their families. For example, supporting research into the causes and treatment of autism can help to improve our understanding of the disorder and promote better outcomes for individuals with autism. Likewise, providing support and resources to families affected by autism can help to reduce the stress and challenges associated with caring for a loved one with the disorder.

Chapter Twenty-Three

Autism in the Workplace

Autism is a neurological condition that can affect an individual's social interaction, communication, and behavior. While autism can present challenges in various aspects of life, it is important to note that many individuals with autism are capable of thriving in the workplace with the right accommodations and support.

In recent years, there has been an increased focus on autism in the workplace, as employers recognize the benefits of neurodiversity and seek to create more inclusive environments. Below we will explore some of the challenges faced by individuals with autism in the workplace and discuss strategies for accommodating and supporting employees with autism.

One of the most significant challenges faced by individuals with autism in the workplace is communication. Many individuals with autism may struggle with verbal communication, making it difficult for them to express their thoughts and ideas. This can lead to misunderstandings and a lack of productivity, as well as frustration on the part of the individual with autism.

To address this challenge, employers can provide alternative communication methods, such as written communication or visual aids. They can also provide training for all employees to understand and appreciate different communication styles. This can create a more inclusive and supportive workplace culture.

Another challenge faced by individuals with autism in the workplace is sensory sensitivities. Many individuals with autism are sensitive to sensory stimuli, such as bright lights or loud noises. This can be overwhelming in a busy office environment and may impact an individual's ability to focus and be productive.

To address this challenge, employers can make modifications to the workplace environment. For example, they can provide noise-cancelling headphones or adjust lighting to create a more calming environment. They can also offer flexible work arrangements, such as remote work, to allow employees with autism to work in an environment that is more comfortable for them.

Social interaction can also be a challenge for individuals with autism in the workplace. Many individuals with autism struggle with social cues and may have difficulty understanding office politics or social norms. This can lead to isolation and a lack of engagement with coworkers.

To address this challenge, employers can provide social skills training for individuals with autism, as well as all employees. This can include training on nonverbal communication, conflict resolution, and teamwork. Employers can also create social opportunities, such as team-building activities or informal gatherings, to facilitate social interaction and build relationships between employees.

Finally, it is important to recognize that individuals with autism have unique strengths and abilities that can benefit the workplace. Many individuals with autism excel in areas such as attention to detail, problem-solving, and creativity. By embracing neurodiversity and providing accommodations and support, employers can create a more diverse and innovative workplace.

Strategies for Job Seekers with Autism

Autism Spectrum Disorder (ASD) is a developmental disorder that affects communication, social interaction, and behavior. Individuals with autism may experience challenges in various areas, including education, daily living, and employment. However, with appropriate support and strategies, people with autism can excel in their careers and become valuable contributors to the workforce.

One of the main challenges faced by job seekers with autism is the job interview process. Traditional interviews, with their emphasis on social skills and communication, can be particularly daunting for individuals with autism. Therefore, alternative interview methods, such as job tryouts or situational assessments, can provide a more accurate representation of an applicant's abilities and help reduce anxiety.

Another important strategy for job seekers with autism is to identify their strengths and interests and seek out job opportunities that align with these areas. Many individuals with autism have particular talents and skills, such as attention to detail, analytical thinking, or creativity, that can be valuable in various industries. By focusing on these strengths and finding jobs that leverage them, individuals with autism can improve their chances of success and job satisfaction.

Employers can also play a crucial role in supporting individuals with autism in the workplace. Creating a welcoming and inclusive work environment, with clear communication and understanding of autism, can help individuals with autism feel comfortable and thrive in their roles. Employers can also provide training and accommodations, such as visual aids or flexible schedules, to support the unique needs of employees with autism.

Additionally, workplace mentoring programs can be particularly beneficial for individuals with autism. Mentors can provide guidance, support, and feedback to help individuals with autism navigate the workplace, build confidence, and develop their skills. These programs can also help employers foster a more inclusive and diverse workforce and improve employee retention rates.

Finally, job seekers with autism can benefit from networking and support groups. Online communities, such as autism-specific job boards and social media groups, can connect job seekers with autism with employers who are committed to diversity and inclusion. Additionally, support groups, such as those offered by local autism organizations or vocational rehabilitation services, can provide valuable resources, information, and peer support to job seekers with autism.

Supporting Autism Inclusion in the Workplace

Autism is a neurological condition that affects communication, social interaction, and behavior. People with autism often face unique challenges in the workplace, but with the right support and accommodations, they can thrive and succeed. Below we will explore strategies for supporting autism inclusion in the workplace.

One key strategy is to promote awareness and understanding of autism among employers and co-workers. This can involve training sessions and informational materials that help demystify the condition and dispel common misconceptions. Employers can also work with autism advocacy groups to learn best practices for accommodating and supporting employees with autism.

Another important strategy is to provide workplace accommodations that address the unique needs of individuals with autism. These might include flexible work schedules, noise-canceling headphones, and designated quiet spaces. Employers can also consider modifying job duties or expectations to better align with the strengths and interests of employees with autism.

Employers can also foster a supportive and inclusive workplace culture. This might involve promoting teamwork, encouraging open communication, and providing regular feedback and recognition. Employers can also work to eliminate bullying, harassment, and discrimination, which can be especially harmful to individuals with autism.

In addition to these strategies, it is also important to recognize the benefits of employing individuals with autism. Many people with autism have unique strengths and abilities that can be highly valuable in the workplace. For example, they may excel in tasks that require attention to detail, strong memory skills, and the ability to focus for extended periods of time. Employers who embrace diversity and inclusion can reap the rewards of a more innovative, productive, and engaged workforce.

Despite these strategies, there are still significant barriers to autism inclusion in the workplace. For example, many employers may be hesitant to hire individuals with autism due to concerns about job performance, accommodations, and liability. Additionally, individuals with autism may struggle to navigate the job search process, advocate for their needs, and effectively communicate their strengths and abilities.

To overcome these challenges, it is important to promote a collaborative and proactive approach to autism inclusion in the workplace. This might involve partnering with autism advocacy organizations to develop targeted employment programs and support services. Employers can also work with individuals with autism to identify and address their specific needs and preferences.

Employers' Responsibilities and Best Practices

Autism is a neurodevelopmental disorder that affects communication, social interaction, and behavior. Individuals with autism often experience difficulties in traditional social settings, including the workplace. However, with the right support and accommodations, people with autism can be successful in the workforce. Below we will discuss the responsibilities and best practices that employers can implement to support autism inclusion in the workplace.

One of the most important responsibilities for employers is to provide a supportive and inclusive work environment. This means creating a workplace culture that values diversity and promotes understanding and acceptance of neurodiverse individuals. Employers can also work to educate their staff about autism and how to communicate and interact effectively with autistic individuals.

Another important responsibility for employers is to provide reasonable accommodations for employees with autism. Accommodations can include modifications to the physical work environment, such as noise-cancelling headphones or a sensory-friendly workspace. Employers can also make accommodations in work assignments, such as providing written instructions or allowing for flexibility in work hours.

Employers can also work to support the professional development and career growth of their employees with autism. This can include offering mentorship programs, professional development opportunities, and career advancement support. Employers can also work to create a workplace culture that recognizes and values the unique skills and strengths that individuals with autism bring to the table.

Another important aspect of supporting autism inclusion in the workplace is to provide clear and effective communication. Employers can work to provide written instructions, clear expectations, and open lines of communication to ensure that employees with autism have the information they need to be successful in their job. Employers can also work to provide feedback in a constructive and supportive manner, recognizing the unique challenges that employees with autism may face.

Finally, employers can work to ensure that their recruitment and hiring practices are inclusive and accessible to individuals with autism. This can include providing clear and accessible job descriptions, offering accommodations during the application and interview process, and partnering with autism advocacy organizations to reach a wider pool of qualified candidates.

In addition to these responsibilities, there are also several best practices that employers can implement to support autism inclusion in the workplace. These best practices include:

Providing training and resources for managers and coworkers on how to effectively communicate and interact with individuals with autism.

Offering flexible work arrangements, such as telecommuting or modified work hours, to accommodate the needs of employees with autism.

Creating a sensory-friendly workspace, including providing noise-cancelling headphones or dimming lights.

Providing written instructions and visual aids to support employees with autism in understanding tasks and assignments.

Encouraging the use of assistive technologies, such as speech-to-text software or visual aids.

Offering mentorship programs and career development support to help employees with autism succeed in their careers.

Partnering with autism advocacy organizations to provide additional resources and support to employees with autism.

Chapter Twenty-Four

Autism and Relationships

Autism spectrum disorder (ASD) affects individuals in various ways, including how they form and maintain relationships. While individuals with autism may experience difficulties with social communication, sensory processing, and emotional regulation, they can also form meaningful connections with others. Below we will explore the challenges and benefits of relationships for individuals with autism, and provide tips for building and maintaining healthy relationships.

Challenges of Relationships for Individuals with Autism

Individuals with autism may struggle to form and maintain relationships due to challenges with social communication and interaction. This can result in difficulties with making friends, dating, and maintaining romantic relationships. These challenges may also lead to social isolation and loneliness, which can negatively impact mental health.

Another challenge for individuals with autism is sensory processing differences. Certain sounds, smells, textures, and other sensory experiences can be overwhelming and uncomfortable, making it difficult to engage in social activities or maintain relationships. Additionally, changes in routine or unexpected events may cause anxiety and stress, leading to difficulties with emotional regulation.

Benefits of Relationships for Individuals with Autism

Despite the challenges, relationships can bring numerous benefits to individuals with autism. Close relationships provide emotional support, reduce feelings of loneliness and social isolation, and increase overall well-being. Research has also shown that positive relationships can lead to better physical health, improved mental health, and increased life satisfaction.

In addition, relationships can provide opportunities for social skills development and practice. Individuals with autism may struggle with social communication and interaction, but with support and practice, they can improve their skills and develop meaningful connections with others.

Tips for Building and Maintaining Healthy Relationships

For individuals with autism, building and maintaining healthy relationships may require additional support and understanding from others. Here are some tips for individuals with autism and those in their lives who want to support them in building and maintaining healthy relationships:

1. Understand the individual's communication and sensory needs: Individuals with autism may communicate and process sensory information differently than others. It is important to understand their specific needs and preferences in order to communicate effectively and create comfortable environments for social interactions.

2. Focus on shared interests: Common interests can provide a foundation for social connections and conversations. Focusing on shared interests can also help individuals with autism feel more comfortable and confident in social situations.

3. Provide clear and explicit communication: Individuals with autism may struggle with understanding social cues and nonverbal communication. Providing clear and explicit communication can help them understand expectations and prevent miscommunication.

4. Allow for flexibility and routine: Changes in routine and unexpected events can be difficult for individuals with autism. Allowing for flexibility while maintaining a general routine can provide a sense of stability and reduce anxiety and stress.

5. Provide support for emotional regulation: Individuals with autism may struggle with emotional regulation. Providing support and strategies for managing emotions can help them navigate social situations and maintain healthy relationships.

6. Seek professional support: Seeking support from professionals, such as therapists or social skills coaches, can provide additional guidance and strategies for building and maintaining healthy relationships.

Building and Maintaining Friendships

Autism is a neurodevelopmental disorder that affects an individual's communication, social interaction, and behavior. One of the most challenging aspects of living with autism can be building and maintaining friendships. However, with the right support and strategies, individuals with autism can develop meaningful and lasting friendships. Below we will explore some strategies for building and maintaining friendships for individuals with autism.

One of the keys to building friendships is developing shared interests and hobbies. For individuals with autism, it may be helpful to focus on interests that are related to their strengths and passions. For example, if an individual with autism has a keen interest in computers, they may want to join a computer club or participate in online communities focused on computer programming or gaming. By joining a community of like-minded individuals, they can develop relationships based on shared interests.

Another way to build friendships is by participating in group activities. Group activities such as sports teams, music groups, and art classes can provide opportunities for social interaction and collaboration with others. These types of activities can also help individuals with autism to develop important social skills, such as turn-taking, sharing, and cooperation.

In addition to participating in group activities, it is also important for individuals with autism to learn and practice social skills. Many individuals with autism struggle with social communication, such as making eye contact or understanding nonverbal cues. Social skills training can help individuals with autism to develop these skills, which can make it easier for them to interact with others and build friendships.

Another important aspect of building friendships for individuals with autism is identifying and managing sensory sensitivities. Many individuals with autism have sensory sensitivities that can make it challenging to participate in group activities or spend time with others. For example, loud noises or bright lights may be overwhelming for some individuals with autism. By identifying and managing sensory sensitivities, individuals with autism can participate more fully in social activities and build friendships with others.

Maintaining friendships can also be challenging for individuals with autism. One strategy that can be helpful is to schedule regular social activities with friends. This can help individuals with autism to maintain their friendships over time and provide opportunities for ongoing social interaction.

Another important strategy for maintaining friendships is to communicate openly and honestly. Individuals with autism may struggle with social communication, but being open and honest about their needs and feelings can help to strengthen their friendships. It is also important for friends and family members to be patient and understanding, as individuals with autism may need more time or support to communicate effectively.

In some cases, individuals with autism may benefit from peer support groups or counseling to help them build and maintain friendships. These types of groups can provide a safe and supportive environment for individuals with autism to develop social skills, practice communication, and share their experiences with others who have similar challenges.

Navigating Romantic Relationships and Dating

Navigating Romantic Relationships and Dating for Individuals with Autism

Autism is a neurodevelopmental disorder that affects social communication and interaction skills. These challenges can make it difficult for individuals with autism to form and maintain romantic relationships. Navigating romantic relationships and dating can be complicated for everyone, but it can be particularly challenging for those on the autism spectrum. However, with the right tools and support, individuals with autism can learn to navigate these challenges and develop meaningful and fulfilling romantic relationships.

One of the primary challenges for individuals with autism in romantic relationships is difficulty with social communication and interaction. They may struggle with interpreting nonverbal cues such as body language and facial expressions and may have difficulty initiating conversations or expressing their thoughts and feelings. They may also have difficulty understanding social norms and may not pick up on subtle cues in romantic situations.

Another challenge is sensory sensitivities. Individuals with autism may be sensitive to certain textures, sounds, smells, and lighting. These sensitivities can be particularly challenging in romantic situations, such as crowded restaurants, movie theaters, or loud music venues.

Despite these challenges, there are strategies that can help individuals with autism navigate romantic relationships and dating. One strategy is to focus on developing strong communication skills. This can involve learning to express thoughts and feelings clearly and directly, as well as learning to listen actively to others. Individuals with autism may benefit from learning how to read nonverbal cues and practicing social skills with a trusted friend or therapist.

Another strategy is to identify and manage sensory sensitivities. This can involve finding ways to mitigate the impact of sensory stimuli, such as using noise-cancelling headphones, bringing a fidget toy to manage anxiety, or choosing quieter or less crowded environments for romantic outings.

It is also important for individuals with autism to establish boundaries and communicate them clearly in romantic relationships. This can involve identifying personal boundaries, such as physical touch or social interactions, and communicating them openly with a partner.

Dating can be challenging for individuals with autism, but there are several strategies that can help make the experience more manageable. One strategy is to start small, such as meeting for coffee or taking a walk in a quiet park. This can help reduce sensory overload and anxiety and provide a comfortable environment for conversation and connection.

Another strategy is to consider online dating, which can provide a structured environment for getting to know someone and communicating openly and directly. Online dating platforms also allow individuals with autism to connect with others who share similar interests and lifestyles.

It is important for individuals with autism to take care of their emotional and mental health when navigating romantic relationships and dating. This can involve seeking support from trusted friends and family members, as well as working with a therapist or counselor who specializes in autism and relationships.

In addition to these strategies, it is important for society to support individuals with autism in developing meaningful and fulfilling romantic relationships. This can involve increasing awareness and understanding of autism and the unique challenges faced by individuals on the spectrum in romantic relationships. It can also involve creating inclusive and supportive communities where individuals with autism can connect with others and find acceptance and understanding.

The Importance of Social Connections for Well-being

The importance of social connections for well-being cannot be overstated. Socializing with others helps to build relationships, provides opportunities for personal growth, and enhances one's sense of belonging and purpose. However, for individuals with autism spectrum disorder (ASD), socializing can be challenging due to difficulties with communication and social interaction.

Research shows that individuals with ASD have a greater risk of experiencing social isolation and loneliness than their neurotypical peers. This can lead to increased rates of anxiety, depression, and other mental health issues. Therefore, it is important to prioritize social connections and support individuals with ASD in building and maintaining them.

One way to support social connections for individuals with ASD is through social skills training. Social skills training can help individuals learn how to initiate and maintain conversations, read social cues, and navigate social situations. This can be done through individual or group therapy, and can be tailored to meet the specific needs of the individual.

In addition to social skills training, it is also important to provide opportunities for socialization in a structured and supportive environment. This can be done through participation in social clubs or groups, such as sports teams or special interest clubs. These groups can provide a sense of belonging and help individuals with ASD to build relationships with peers who share their interests.

Another important aspect of social connections for individuals with ASD is the support of family and caregivers. Family members and caregivers can play an important role in helping individuals with ASD build and maintain social connections by providing guidance and support in social situations, and by facilitating opportunities for socialization.

Furthermore, technology can also play a role in supporting social connections for individuals with ASD. Social media and other online platforms can provide opportunities for individuals with ASD to connect with others who share their interests and experiences. However, it is important to monitor online interactions to ensure safety and appropriate behavior.

Chapter Twenty-Five

The Role of Support Animals in Autism

The use of support animals, such as therapy dogs, has been increasingly recognized as a beneficial intervention for individuals with various disabilities, including autism. Autism is a complex developmental disorder that affects social interaction, communication, and behavior. While there is no cure for autism, various treatments and interventions have been developed to support individuals with autism and improve their quality of life. In recent years, the use of support animals has gained attention as a non-pharmacological and complementary intervention for individuals with autism. Below we will explore the benefits of support animals for individuals with autism and the various types of support animals that can be utilized.

Firstly, it is important to understand that support animals, also known as emotional support animals (ESAs), are different from service animals. Service animals are trained to perform specific tasks to assist individuals with disabilities, such as guide dogs for individuals who are visually impaired. On the other hand, ESAs are animals that provide emotional support, comfort, and companionship to individuals with emotional or mental health conditions, including autism. ESAs are not required to have specialized training, unlike service animals.

Research has shown that support animals can have positive effects on individuals with autism. For example, a study conducted by the University of Missouri found that children with autism who had a support dog had improved social skills and decreased levels of problem behavior compared to children without a support dog. The study also found that having a support dog was associated with increased positive social behaviors, such as sharing, helping, and cooperating.

Moreover, support animals can also provide emotional comfort and a sense of security to individuals with autism. For some individuals with autism, the presence of a support animal can help reduce anxiety and stress in unfamiliar or overwhelming situations. Support animals can also provide a calming influence and help individuals with autism regulate their emotions.

While dogs are the most commonly used support animals for individuals with autism, other types of animals can also be utilized. For example, horses have been used in equine-assisted therapy, which involves interacting with horses in a structured and supervised environment. This type of therapy has been shown to improve social skills, communication, and self-esteem in individuals with autism.

Additionally, small animals such as cats, rabbits, and guinea pigs can also provide emotional support to individuals with autism. These animals are often low-maintenance and can be easily incorporated into daily routines. Research has shown that interactions with animals, even for brief periods of time, can lead to decreased levels of stress and increased feelings of well-being.

In order to receive the benefits of support animals, it is important to carefully consider the individual's needs and preferences, as well as the animal's temperament and compatibility with the individual. It is also important to work with a qualified professional, such as a licensed therapist or animal behaviorist, to determine the appropriate type of animal and the best ways to incorporate it into the individual's treatment plan.

Furthermore, it is important to note that the use of support animals for individuals with autism is not a substitute for other evidence-based interventions, such as behavioral therapy and medication management. Rather, support animals can be used as a complementary intervention to support the individual's overall well-being and treatment plan.

Benefits of Assistance and Therapy Animals

Assistance and therapy animals have become increasingly popular in recent years for their ability to improve the lives of people with various disabilities and conditions, including autism. These animals can provide a range of benefits, from emotional support to increased independence and social skills. Below we will explore the benefits of assistance and therapy animals for individuals with autism.

Assistance animals are trained to help their owners with specific tasks, while therapy animals are used in a therapeutic setting to provide comfort and emotional support. Both types of animals can be helpful for individuals with autism, depending on their individual needs.

One of the primary benefits of assistance and therapy animals is their ability to provide emotional support. Many individuals with autism struggle with anxiety, depression, and other mental health issues. Assistance and therapy animals can provide comfort and companionship, reducing stress and anxiety levels.

Assistance animals can also help individuals with autism become more independent. Service dogs, for example, can be trained to perform tasks such as retrieving items, opening doors, and alerting their owners to potential dangers. This increased independence can boost confidence and self-esteem, leading to an overall improvement in well-being.

In addition to emotional support and increased independence, assistance and therapy animals can also help individuals with autism develop social skills. Socializing can be challenging for many people with autism, but animals can provide a low-pressure environment for social interaction. This can lead to improved communication and socialization skills, which can carry over into other areas of life.

Assistance and therapy animals can also provide a sense of routine and predictability. Many individuals with autism benefit from structure and predictability in their daily lives, and animals can provide this. The daily routine of caring for an animal can be comforting and grounding, providing a sense of stability in an otherwise uncertain world.

Research has shown that assistance and therapy animals can have a positive impact on individuals with autism. One study found that therapy dogs can increase social interaction and communication in children with autism. Another study found that the presence of a therapy dog can reduce stress levels in individuals with autism during medical procedures.

It is important to note that not all individuals with autism will benefit from assistance or therapy animals. Each person is unique, and it is important to consider their individual needs and preferences when deciding whether an animal is right for them. Additionally, not all animals are suitable for assistance or therapy work. Proper training and certification is necessary to ensure that the animal is safe and effective in its role.

Selecting and Training an Autism Support Animal

Selecting and Training an Autism Support Animal

Autism Spectrum Disorder (ASD) is a neurodevelopmental disorder that affects communication, behavior, and social interaction. People with ASD may find it challenging to navigate certain situations, including social interactions, sensory overload, and emotional regulation. One way to support individuals with ASD is by having an autism support animal. These animals are trained to provide emotional support, reduce anxiety, and assist with sensory needs. However, selecting and training an autism support animal requires careful consideration to ensure the animal is a good match for the individual with ASD.

Selecting an Autism Support Animal:

When selecting an autism support animal, it is essential to consider the individual's needs and preferences. Some individuals may prefer a particular type of animal, such as a dog or a cat, while others may prefer a non-traditional animal such as a rabbit or a bird. Factors to consider when selecting an autism support animal include the individual's lifestyle, living situation, and any allergies or phobias.

It is also essential to consider the temperament of the animal. Autism support animals must be well-behaved, calm, and friendly. Temperament testing is often done to ensure that the animal is suitable for service work. Furthermore, animals that are easily stressed, aggressive, or have a history of biting are not suitable for service work.

Training an Autism Support Animal:

1. Training an autism support animal requires patience, consistency, and a well-thought-out plan. Training typically involves two phases: obedience training and task training. Obedience training teaches the animal basic commands such as "sit," "stay," and "come." Task training teaches the animal specific skills that will assist the individual with ASD.

Some common tasks that an autism support animal can be trained to do include:

2. Sensory Support: Many individuals with ASD experience sensory overload. An autism support animal can be trained to interrupt and redirect the individual's attention away from a trigger.

3. Emotional Support: An autism support animal can provide emotional support by offering comfort, reducing anxiety, and providing a sense of security.

4. Social Interaction: Autism support animals can be trained to assist with social interaction by helping the individual navigate social situations and building connections.

5. Safety Support: An autism support animal can be trained to alert the individual or a caregiver to potential danger, such as traffic or seizures.

It is important to note that training an autism support animal is a long process that requires ongoing reinforcement and repetition. It is also essential to have a qualified and experienced trainer to ensure that the animal is trained correctly and is suitable for service work.

Legal Rights and Responsibilities for Support Animals

Legal Rights and Responsibilities for Support Animals

Support animals can play a critical role in the lives of individuals with autism. They can provide emotional support, reduce stress and anxiety, and help improve social interactions. However, when it comes to legal rights and responsibilities for support animals, there is a lot of confusion and misinformation. Below we will explore the legal framework for support animals and what rights and responsibilities owners have.

The Americans with Disabilities Act (ADA) is a federal law that protects the rights of people with disabilities, including those who use support animals. Under the ADA, people with disabilities are allowed to bring their support animals into public places, such as restaurants, hotels, and stores. This law also applies to public transportation, including buses, trains, and airplanes. This means that individuals with autism who use support animals can travel with their animals without fear of discrimination.

To qualify for the protections of the ADA, a support animal must be trained to perform a specific task related to the owner's disability. For individuals with autism, this could include tasks such as interrupting self-injurious behaviors, alerting to impending meltdowns, or providing calming pressure during times of distress. The animal must also be well-behaved in public and not pose a threat to the health or safety of others.

It is important to note that the ADA only applies to service animals, which are defined as dogs or, in some cases, miniature horses. Emotional support animals (ESAs) do not qualify as service animals under the ADA, and therefore do not have the same legal protections. While ESAs can provide emotional support to their owners, they are not trained to perform specific tasks related to a disability.

Despite not being considered service animals under the ADA, ESAs are still protected under other laws, including the Fair Housing Act (FHA). This law requires housing providers to allow tenants with disabilities to have their ESAs in their homes, even if the building has a no-pets policy. This applies to both rented and owned homes, as well as public housing.

To qualify for an ESA, the owner must have a diagnosed disability, and the animal must provide emotional support that alleviates one or more symptoms of the disability. The animal does not need to be trained to perform a specific task, but must still be well-behaved in public and not pose a threat to others.

It is important to note that there are limitations to these protections. Landlords and housing providers are not required to allow ESAs if the animal would cause an undue financial burden or fundamentally alter the nature of the housing provider's business. Additionally, ESAs are not allowed in public places under the ADA.

Another important consideration for support animal owners is their responsibilities. While they have the right to bring their animals into public places and housing, they also have a responsibility to ensure their animals are well-behaved and not a threat to others. This includes ensuring the animal is properly trained and controlled, and that it is kept clean and healthy.

In the case of ESAs, owners must provide documentation from a healthcare professional that verifies their disability and the need for an ESA. This documentation should be provided to housing providers or landlords upon request.

Chapter Twenty-Six

Autism and Aging

Autism spectrum disorder (ASD) is a lifelong neurodevelopmental condition that affects communication, social interaction, and behavior. As individuals with ASD age, they may experience unique challenges and needs that require specific attention and support. It is essential to understand these challenges and create strategies that promote positive outcomes for aging individuals with ASD.

The prevalence of autism in older adults is not well understood due to the limited research in this area. However, recent studies suggest that the number of adults with autism is increasing, and the number of aging individuals with autism is likely to grow in the future. This growth in the aging population with autism highlights the need for increased awareness and support.

One of the significant challenges for aging individuals with autism is social isolation. Individuals with autism may have difficulty in socializing and forming friendships, leading to limited social networks. Aging can exacerbate this issue as many individuals experience changes in social support networks due to death or relocation. Therefore, individuals with autism need social support that can help them build new relationships and maintain existing ones.

Another challenge for aging individuals with autism is physical health. Studies have shown that individuals with autism have a higher prevalence of medical conditions, including gastrointestinal problems, epilepsy, and sleep disorders. Additionally, individuals with autism may have difficulty in communicating their health needs and symptoms, leading to inadequate medical care. Therefore, it is crucial to provide healthcare that addresses the unique needs of individuals with autism.

Cognitive decline is another issue that aging individuals with autism may face. Studies have shown that older adults with autism may experience a decline in cognitive abilities, leading to difficulties in daily living activities. Therefore, it is important to provide appropriate support, such as cognitive training and occupational therapy, to help aging individuals with autism maintain their independence.

Housing is another critical issue for aging individuals with autism. Many individuals with autism live in residential facilities or with family members, but as they age, their needs for housing may change. Aging individuals with autism may require accessible housing with accommodations for their specific needs. Additionally, housing options need to be available that allow aging individuals with autism to maintain their independence while receiving the necessary support.

Employment and financial security are also essential considerations for aging individuals with autism. As individuals with autism age, their ability to maintain employment may decline, leading to financial insecurity. It is essential to provide support and vocational training to help aging individuals with autism maintain their employment and financial independence.

Addressing the Unique Needs of Aging Adults with Autism

Autism is a lifelong neurodevelopmental condition that affects social communication, behavior, and sensory processing. As individuals with autism age, they may experience unique challenges and needs. It is important to address these challenges to ensure that individuals with autism can age with dignity and receive the appropriate support they require.

One of the challenges faced by aging adults with autism is the lack of appropriate housing options. Many individuals with autism require specialized living arrangements that meet their unique needs. For example, some may require quiet environments, while others may require specialized sensory rooms. It is important to provide safe and supportive housing options that meet the specific needs of individuals with autism as they age.

Another challenge faced by aging adults with autism is social isolation. Many individuals with autism have difficulty with social communication and making connections with others, which can lead to loneliness and social isolation. It is important to provide opportunities for social engagement and connection, such as support groups, social clubs, and other community-based activities.

In addition to social isolation, aging adults with autism may experience difficulties with healthcare. Many healthcare providers may not have experience working with individuals with autism, which can make it challenging to provide appropriate care. It is important to educate healthcare providers on the unique needs of individuals with autism, including sensory processing issues, communication challenges, and behavioral concerns.

As individuals with autism age, they may also experience changes in their sensory processing abilities. Some individuals may become more sensitive to certain sensory stimuli, while others may experience decreased sensitivity. It is important to provide appropriate accommodations, such as adjusting lighting or sound levels, to ensure that individuals with autism can comfortably navigate their environments.

Finally, as individuals with autism age, they may experience changes in their behavior. Some individuals may develop new or worsening behavioral challenges, such as anxiety or aggression. It is important to provide appropriate support and interventions to address these challenges, such as cognitive-behavioral therapy or medication management.

Planning for Long-term Care and Support

Autism is a lifelong developmental condition that affects communication, social interaction, and behavior. As individuals with autism age, their support needs may change and increase, making planning for long-term care and support crucial. Below we will explore the importance of planning for long-term care and support for aging adults with autism.

Firstly, it is essential to understand that aging adults with autism have unique needs. According to research, individuals with autism have a higher risk of developing co-occurring medical conditions, such as epilepsy, gastrointestinal issues, and sleep disorders, as they age. These conditions may require specialized medical care, which can be expensive and may not be covered by insurance. Additionally, as individuals with autism age, they may experience difficulties with mobility, which can make it challenging to access healthcare services or participate in social activities. It is, therefore, important to ensure that adequate support and resources are available to meet their changing needs.

Planning for long-term care and support involves identifying the necessary resources and services that will be required to meet the needs of aging adults with autism. One of the most critical resources is housing. Many individuals with autism may require specialized housing that meets their unique needs. For example, some may require 24-hour support, while others may need a quieter living environment. It is important to plan for appropriate housing well in advance to ensure that it meets the individual's needs and provides a safe and comfortable living environment.

Another crucial aspect of long-term care and support is financial planning. It is important to consider the cost of specialized care and support services and how they will be funded. In many cases, families may need to seek financial assistance from government programs or nonprofit organizations. It is essential to research the available resources and plan accordingly to ensure that the individual with autism receives the necessary care and support.

Additionally, long-term care planning should include considerations for legal and financial decision-making. As individuals with autism age, they may become less capable of making important decisions independently. It is, therefore, crucial to plan for legal and financial decision-making, such as creating a power of attorney or guardianship agreement, to ensure that the individual's interests are protected.

In addition to these practical considerations, it is also essential to plan for social and emotional support. Aging adults with autism may experience social isolation and loneliness, which can negatively impact their mental health and well-being. It is, therefore, important to identify opportunities for social engagement and ensure that the individual has access to activities and programs that align with their interests and abilities.

Strategies for Maintaining Quality of Life in Later Years

As individuals with autism age, they may face unique challenges that can impact their quality of life. These challenges can include physical and cognitive decline, difficulty accessing appropriate healthcare, social isolation, and changes in living arrangements. However, with appropriate planning and support, individuals with autism can maintain a high quality of life in their later years.

One important strategy for maintaining quality of life in later years is to establish a comprehensive care plan. This plan should consider the individual's medical, social, and emotional needs and outline specific steps for addressing each area. For example, the plan may include regular medical check-ups, therapy sessions, and social activities to promote engagement and prevent isolation.

Another key strategy is to ensure that the individual has access to appropriate healthcare. This can be challenging for individuals with autism, as they may have difficulty communicating their needs and may require specialized care. It is important to work with healthcare providers who have experience working with individuals with autism and who can provide the necessary accommodations to ensure that the individual receives high-quality care.

In addition, social support is crucial for maintaining quality of life in later years. This can include engaging in activities that promote social interaction and connection, such as joining social groups or participating in hobbies that involve other people. It can also involve seeking out support from family members, friends, or professionals who can provide emotional support and guidance.

It is also important to consider changes in living arrangements as individuals with autism age. This may involve modifying their current living situation to accommodate physical or cognitive changes, or it may involve transitioning to a new living arrangement that better meets their needs. For example, an individual may choose to move into a retirement community that provides specialized support for individuals with autism.

Finally, financial planning is also an important consideration for maintaining quality of life in later years. This may involve establishing a long-term financial plan that considers the individual's current and future needs and identifies resources that can help support them as they age.

Chapter Twenty-Seven

Celebrating Neurodiversity

Neurodiversity is the concept that neurological differences such as autism, ADHD, dyslexia, and others are natural variations in the human experience rather than disorders to be cured. It is a movement that promotes the idea that we should embrace and celebrate the diversity of human brains and the unique perspectives that come with them. The neurodiversity movement is a call for understanding, acceptance, and inclusivity of individuals with neurodivergent conditions. Below we will explore the concept of neurodiversity and why it is essential to celebrate and embrace it.

Neurodiversity challenges the notion that there is a "normal" brain and that any deviation from that is abnormal. Instead, it recognizes that the human brain is incredibly complex and diverse, and that there are many different ways of processing information and experiencing the world. Neurodiversity advocates believe that neurological differences should be respected, accommodated, and valued, rather than stigmatized and pathologized.

One of the key benefits of embracing neurodiversity is that it encourages us to see the strengths and positive qualities that come with neurodivergent conditions. For example, people with autism are often highly analytical, detail-oriented, and can have a unique perspective on the world. Those with ADHD can be highly creative, innovative, and energetic. When we focus on these strengths, we can help individuals with neurodivergent conditions develop their talents and abilities to their full potential.

Another benefit of embracing neurodiversity is that it promotes inclusivity and helps to break down the barriers that can prevent people with neurodivergent conditions from fully participating in society. By recognizing and accommodating the different ways that people process information and experience the world, we can create environments that are more accessible and welcoming to everyone.

Unfortunately, there is still a significant amount of stigma and discrimination associated with neurodivergent conditions. Many people with these conditions face challenges in accessing education, employment, and healthcare. Embracing neurodiversity means challenging these stigmas and fighting for the rights of neurodivergent individuals to be fully included in society.

One way to celebrate and embrace neurodiversity is to focus on creating more neurodiverse-friendly environments. This includes creating sensory-friendly spaces that are less overwhelming and more accommodating for those with sensory sensitivities, as well as providing accommodations like extended time for exams or the use of assistive technology.

Another way to embrace neurodiversity is to focus on education and awareness. This includes educating people about the strengths and positive qualities associated with neurodivergent conditions, as well as educating people about the challenges that those with these conditions face. It also means promoting acceptance and understanding of those who think differently than we do.

Finally, it is essential to recognize that neurodiversity is not just about those with clinically diagnosed conditions. It is about recognizing that everyone has a unique way of thinking and experiencing the world. By embracing this diversity, we can create a more inclusive and compassionate society for all.

Embracing the Strengths and Talents of Individuals with Autism

Autism is a neurodevelopmental disorder that affects individuals in various ways. While it is often associated with challenges in social communication and interactions, repetitive behaviors, and sensory processing, autism is also characterized by unique strengths and talents. Individuals with autism can have exceptional abilities in areas such as visual thinking, memory, attention to detail, and pattern recognition.

Embracing the strengths and talents of individuals with autism is essential for creating a more inclusive and diverse society. The concept of neurodiversity recognizes that differences in brain function and behavior are normal and that individuals with neurological differences such as autism have unique perspectives and abilities that should be valued and celebrated.

One of the strengths often associated with autism is visual thinking. Many individuals with autism have exceptional spatial reasoning skills and are able to think in pictures. This can be a valuable asset in fields such as engineering, architecture, and design. In fact, some of the most innovative and successful designers and architects in history, such as Michelangelo and Frank Lloyd Wright, are thought to have had traits of autism.

Attention to detail is another common strength among individuals with autism. Many have an ability to focus on specific details that others may miss, which can be beneficial in fields such as science and technology. Some individuals with autism have a remarkable ability to remember specific facts and details, which can also be an asset in fields such as history and literature.

Another strength associated with autism is creativity. Many individuals with autism have a unique way of thinking and seeing the world that can lead to innovative and creative solutions. Some individuals with autism have a particular talent for music, art, or other forms of creative expression.

It is essential to recognize and value the strengths and talents of individuals with autism, as doing so can help them to achieve their full potential and contribute to society in meaningful ways. It is also important to create opportunities for individuals with autism to use their strengths and talents in education, employment, and other areas of life.

One way to embrace the strengths of individuals with autism is to focus on their abilities rather than their disabilities. This means identifying and supporting their strengths and interests, rather than solely focusing on areas of weakness or challenge. It also means providing accommodations and support that enable individuals with autism to use their strengths in education and employment settings.

Another way to embrace the strengths of individuals with autism is to promote neurodiversity in the workplace. This means recognizing and valuing the unique perspectives and abilities of individuals with autism and other neurological differences. It also means creating a workplace culture that is inclusive and accommodating of neurodiverse individuals.

In education settings, embracing the strengths of individuals with autism means creating opportunities for them to use their strengths and interests in learning. This may involve providing visual aids and other materials that cater to their visual thinking abilities or incorporating music and art into the curriculum to tap into their creativity.

Promoting Autism Acceptance and Inclusion

Autism, a neurodevelopmental disorder, affects individuals differently and can present unique challenges. Historically, autism has been stigmatized, misunderstood, and approached through the lens of deficit and pathology. However, a growing movement has emerged to promote autism acceptance and inclusion, recognizing the strengths and talents of individuals with autism. Below we will explore the importance of promoting autism acceptance and inclusion, and the ways in which society can work towards this goal.

Firstly, promoting autism acceptance and inclusion is essential to combatting the stigma that often surrounds autism. In the past, autism was often viewed as a disease that needed to be cured, and individuals with autism were viewed as burdens on society. This perception has led to discrimination and marginalization, preventing individuals with autism from fully participating in society. However, promoting autism acceptance and inclusion can help to counteract this negative perception, leading to greater understanding and acceptance of those with autism.

Secondly, promoting autism acceptance and inclusion is important because it can lead to better outcomes for individuals with autism. When individuals with autism feel accepted and valued, they are more likely to have positive self-esteem, which can lead to better mental health outcomes. Additionally, when individuals with autism are included in society, they have more opportunities to learn and grow, which can lead to greater independence and a higher quality of life.

There are several ways that society can work towards promoting autism acceptance and inclusion. One way is through education and awareness campaigns. Educating the public about autism and its unique challenges can help to break down stereotypes and promote understanding. Additionally, individuals with autism can be involved in these campaigns to share their experiences and help to promote a more positive perception of autism.

Another way to promote autism acceptance and inclusion is through creating more accessible environments. For example, workplaces can create accommodations for individuals with autism, such as providing quiet spaces or allowing for flexible work schedules. Schools can also make accommodations for students with autism, such as providing sensory breaks or offering alternative forms of communication. By creating more accessible environments, individuals with autism can more fully participate in society and feel valued and included.

Finally, promoting autism acceptance and inclusion can also involve celebrating the strengths and talents of individuals with autism. Rather than solely focusing on deficits and challenges, society can recognize the unique abilities and contributions that individuals with autism can bring to the table. For example, many individuals with autism have exceptional visual-spatial skills or excel in areas such as music or math. By celebrating these strengths and talents, society can help to promote a more positive perception of autism and encourage greater inclusion.

Fostering a Neurodiverse Society for All

Fostering a Neurodiverse Society for All

Autism is a neurological condition that affects individuals in various ways, with each person experiencing their own unique set of strengths and challenges. For a long time, autism was misunderstood and stigmatized, leading to discrimination and marginalization of individuals with autism. However, in recent years, there has been a growing movement towards neurodiversity, which recognizes and embraces the unique perspectives and abilities of individuals with autism and other neurological differences.

Below we will explore the importance of fostering a neurodiverse society for all and the ways in which we can achieve this goal.

One of the main benefits of embracing neurodiversity is that it creates a more inclusive society. When we recognize the strengths and abilities of individuals with autism and other neurological differences, we are more likely to provide them with the support and resources they need to thrive. This can include accommodations in the workplace, educational settings, and other areas of life. For example, individuals with autism may benefit from visual aids, social stories, and other tools that help them navigate social situations and communicate effectively.

Moreover, a neurodiverse society benefits everyone, not just individuals with autism. Embracing neurodiversity means recognizing that different people have different ways of thinking, processing information, and experiencing the world. This can lead to more innovative and creative problem-solving, as individuals with different perspectives and approaches can work together to find solutions. Additionally, a more diverse workforce can bring a wider range of skills and experiences to the table, leading to better outcomes and more successful companies.

So, how can we foster a more neurodiverse society? One important step is to increase awareness and understanding of autism and other neurological differences. This can be achieved through education and advocacy, such as hosting workshops and events that promote understanding and acceptance of neurodiversity. It also involves challenging stereotypes and misconceptions about autism and other neurological differences. For instance, rather than viewing autism as a disability, we should recognize that it is simply a different way of processing information and experiencing the world.

Another important step is to provide individuals with autism and other neurological differences with the support and resources they need to succeed. This can involve accommodations in the workplace, such as flexible schedules and quiet workspaces, or accommodations in educational settings, such as extended time on tests and assignments. Additionally, it can involve providing access to therapies and interventions that help individuals with autism develop the skills they need to thrive in various areas of life.

It is also important to involve individuals with autism and other neurological differences in discussions about how to create a more neurodiverse society. This means listening to their perspectives and experiences and incorporating their ideas and feedback into policies and practices. Additionally, it involves providing individuals with autism with opportunities to contribute to society in meaningful ways, such as through employment or volunteer work.

9781776968961
SD - #0050 - 121026 - C0 - 229/152/13 - PB - 9781776968961 - Matt Lamination